STRONGER THAN DE

STRONGER THAN DEATH

A Study of Love for the Dying

Roland Riem

Foreword by Rowan Williams

I am the resurrection.
Anyone who believes in me,
even though that person dies,
will live,
and whoever lives and believes in me
will never die.
(John 11:25f)

DARTON · LONGMAN + TODD

First published in 1993 by
Darton Longman and Todd Ltd
1 Spencer Court
140–142 Wandsworth High Street
London SW18 4JJ

ISBN 0–232–51991–9

A catalogue record for this book is available
from the British Library

Phototypeset by Intype, London
Printed and bound in Great Britain
at the University Press, Cambridge

In loving memory of Rosalie
whose life and death gave birth to this book

CONTENTS

FOREWORD

The simple but fundamental insight that lies at the heart of this book is that pastoral care is about the creation of community; and this insight is here tested against the pastoral situation where this model is hardest to apply, the care of the dying. How do we create a real community with those who are just not going to be there as active participants in any community we can sense or understand? Part of the answer is found in what the dying themselves minister – the knowledge that truth and life are found in letting go, and that communion that endures is on the other side of silence and loss, loss of solutions, loss of a visible future, loss of words to master things with. To confront death is to confront our bodily being, in all its frailty and dumbness, to recognise what touch says that talk can't. To live from that level is to live from God's self-giving.

Hence the importance of John's Gospel as a pastoral resource in these pages. The Christ of St John lives from the depths of God; and we are shown how deeply we misunderstand John if we read him as minimising the vulnerability of Jesus. John's Jesus, dramatically and repeatedly, refuses to make any claim for himself but that he is the one who stands aside so that God and the human world may meet in truth, and this 'stepping aside' is the centre of his action and his Passion. The pastor and the dying person can both look to this 'standing-aside' to learn the nature of the work they must do together, for each other.

This is a relatively brief book, but it ranges widely and cuts deeply. It is constantly earthed in the author's concrete experience as a counsellor and pastor (and human being), and these pages are illuminated repeatedly by poignant, funny, illuminating stories, far more than just anecdotes. It deploys confidently and movingly the riches of the New Testament; any reader turning back to John's Gospel after reading this book will find practically every page given new significance. And the moral for an impatient and greedy society is bluntly drawn: the hospice becomes an 'alternative community', posing frankly political challenges to the way we do our public business.

The need to revalue and reimagine what it is to take *time* with and for each other is spelled out with authority. It is a book to read in just such a way – taking time, making personal connections – and to read more than once. And while it has obvious importance for those directly concerned with the terminally ill and incurable, any thoughtful Christian can read it with enormous profit and gratitude. It is a model of pastoral theology managing to be both concrete and reflective.

ROWAN WILLIAMS

PREFACE

This book paints a picture. Its central subject is a meeting of two people who have been brought together because one is terminally ill. The one who is dying we shall call the 'patient', not out of a desire to subtract from that person's humanity but because often meetings like this take place at a bed in a hospital or hospice, with medics on call and in control. The label therefore reflects the way we deal with death in our society; it also allows us to avoid defining a living person with a term equally applicable to all. It is not much easier to find a word to describe the one who comes to be beside the patient. 'Carer' sounds too general and 'minister' too ecclesiastical. As the sort of meeting we shall explore is normally called 'pastoral', it is best to stick with 'pastor', despite its paternalist, not to say agricultural, overtones. The main subject of the picture, then, is the meeting between patient and pastor.

Anyone who has tried to write will know that the creative process is a deeply mysterious one. It is a mistake to try to tie down too exactly the origin of certain thoughts. Nonetheless, the reader may better appreciate the meaning of the book if I explain the history behind it. The book is a complete revision and expansion of a dissertation written in the final year of my training for ordained ministry in the Church of England. The dissertation attempted to use the 'Prologue' of John's Gospel (1:1–18) as a way of connecting some ideas from the rest of the Gospel with my first exposure to death and dying, which I had on a two-week placement at Hayward House, City Hospital, Nottingham. All may well have ended there but for my first wife Rosalie's being killed in a road accident, while moving into our new home in Deal. After her

death, through the encouragement and interest of friends, I
started to study for this book, feeling that I had some further
insight to offer a wider audience. This book is dedicated to
her memory with gratitude, not only for the eighteen months
of marriage God gave us but also for her continuing prayer
for the friends she left in the world, which has born fruit in
abundance.

Much has had to be changed. The original work was focussed through the use of the Prologue. Traces of this remain,
though I have now ranged more broadly through the Gospel,
especially concentrating on the events surrounding the Passion. I have also tried to write from a more practical angle
than previously, building into the text such experience of
ministry as I have had since ordination. Along the way I have
received help from many, all of whom cannot, unfortunately,
be named here. I would like to thank the Revd Toby March-
and and the people of the parish of St Leonard's Deal for
their forbearance as I hid myself away to ponder and write.
Special thanks are due to the team at Darton, Longman
and Todd, especially to their Editorial Director, Mary Jean
Pritchard. Her friendly interest and wisdom made the writing
of this book a happy task. The Revd Gordon Oliver has
continued his oversight over my education since I left his
care as Director of Pastoral Studies at St John's College,
Nottingham. As a reader for DLT, he has lent his pastoral
acumen to the study of the whole manuscript, much improv-
ing the quality of the text by his critical comments. I admit
that the blunders in style and content which remain are mine!

I am honoured that one of the pastoral theologians whom
I most admire has been involved in the final production of
this book. My thanks go to the Rt Revd Rowan Williams for
his generous introduction. I am also hugely grateful to my
wife Sophie for allowing her interpretation of the Rublev icon
of the Trinity to be broadcast. I would be delighted if, in this
instance, readers were to judge a book by its cover!

As I was finishing this three-year project I chanced upon
the final chapter of *The Pastoral Act*, by Julia Gatta, a survey
of spiritual guidance in the English mystics. Her words

reassure me that the path I have tried to follow has already been trodden by Christians of great holiness:

> In our contemporary idiom, a 'pastoral' approach in ministry has come to suggest a 'non-judgemental' acceptance of another's standpoint coupled with a 'willingness to be helpful'. This line of thinking is utterly foreign to the English mystics. Though their pastoral practice is authentically compassionate, their love has theological toughness and prophetic strength. Because they have seen God in vision and heard his voice, they can, like the prophets of ancient Israel, distinguish between true and bogus spirituality. . . Only truth can finally comfort.[1]

My hope is that, despite the many imperfections of an over-ruminated book, the reader will be drawn closer to this vision of truth, about which John wrote with such majestic simplicity and which is lived out with equal grace within the modern hospice movement. All royalties from the sale of this book will go to Helen House, Oxford, whose work with terminally ill children and their families exemplifies everything I wish to say in the following chapters, and more besides.

ACKNOWLEDGEMENTS

The scriptural quotations are taken from the New Jerusalem Bible published and copyright 1985 by Darton, Longman and Todd Ltd and Doubleday & Co Inc. and used by permission of the publishers. I am also grateful to David Higham Associates for permission to quote from 'Dust' and 'Let Things Alone' from *Collected Poems* by Elizabeth Jennings published by Carcanet and from 'Do not go gentle into that good night' from *Poems* by Dylan Thomas published by Dent.

1

THE JOURNEY IN TIME TO ETERNITY

Terminally ill people have a journey to make. The tide of time threatens to drown all past and present experience, and every hope for the future. This introductory chapter lays down some markers on the way through the gathering darkness. Because time is running out for the terminally ill, they must discover a different quality of time in which to dwell safely. This can be found in St John's vision of the divine communion which was in the beginning coming into the world in Jesus Christ. Those looking for light must hear his word and follow him through suffering to find rest. The journey is costly, and yet the total threat of death to body and mind can only be met when a patient is prepared to let go of old securities and to trust in God, allowing the Holy Spirit to bring new identity to birth in the human heart. Two stories from a hospice illustrate what must and can happen to those who face death.

The second part of the chapter is devoted to laying theoretical foundations. Readers who wish to concentrate on practical aspects of pastoral care may prefer to treat it as a parenthesis. But before returning to pastoral practice in greater detail the question has to be asked of whether one can legitimately use texts from an ancient book as a pastoral resource in modern and specific contexts. We find that, despite the reservations of some, scriptural images may be taken and applied imaginatively to new situations, when they are interpreted sensitively.

The chapter ends with an overview of the rest of the book.

In the Beginning

> In the beginning was the Word:
> the Word was with God
> and the Word was God.
> He was with God in the beginning. (1:1,2)

These first words of St John's Gospel are also a fitting way to start a study of love for the dying. The 'Prologue' of the Gospel is neither 'a philosophical rationale of the main thesis of the Gospel' nor 'a summary plot of the whole book' nor 'a bare outline of the world-view which is filled in in the rest of the Gospel'.[1] Rather, it invites its reader to see the light of Christ and to share in his glory. John is not speculating about a realm existing apart from the world;[2] he begins his Gospel by proclaiming the revelation of God in Jesus Christ. Into the world's time, its history, the eternal God has come, showing that time and history are fulfilled in him.

The orthodox theologian Paul Evdokimov elucidates this truth with some useful distinctions between different forms of time.[3] There is *cyclical* or *mathematical* time, the time of the clock, measured in hours, minutes and seconds; there is *historical* time, the time of the story, measured in periods, phases and stages; and *existential* time, the time of experience, which is the fulfilment or redemption of the other forms of time. We could call it the time of the eternal moment – sacred, sacramental or liturgical time. The Prologue presents a vision of eternal and unbroken communion, where God is with his Word, coming into the world and shining in the darkness. God's glory has been revealed. It says that there is no need to escape time to reach eternity because Christ has brought the fulfilment of time into the world, in his eternal communion with the Father. John conveys this in the way he constructs the beginning of his Gospel, which Lesslie Newbigin describes in his aptly named commentary, *The Light has Come*: 'The timeless sayings of the Prologue are deliberately not separated from but intertwined with narration of history, because it is in this history that the eternal reality of God is present, active, and manifest.'[4]

So the fulfilment of the world's time dwells in Jesus Christ. He is the gate to the Father, and meeting him is a meeting with eternity. What has been from the beginning is also *now*, when Jesus brings from the Father what humanity needs and what the Father has given his son, eternal life. The hour of Jesus, which has brought this fulfilment of time, is when Jesus is lifted up on the cross, and if in order to express the truth John commends to his readers tenses have to be muddled up, this is because the different forms of time we have described co-inhere.[5] As R.E. Brown has noticed, there is a 'strange timelessness or indifference to normal time' found in verses like 3:13 and 4:38.[6] Mathematical and historical time find their rest in Christ's cry from the cross, 'It is fulfilled'.

More needs to be said about the hour of Jesus before we turn to the temporal needs of hospice patients. John guards against the thought that meeting Jesus can be achieved by religious or moral effort. From the beginning, it is the Word who is with God. Without him nothing would be made and nothing could be remade at all. The Word made flesh does not bring life by encouraging an escape from the threat of passing time or by denying human history of weakness and suffering; instead, his command is to follow. By obeying the call of God in time, by offering their whole history to him, the Word's followers transcend both time and history in their hour, in an eternal moment of communion with their Father.

Rublev's icon of the Holy Trinity illustrates what I have been saying. It expresses, so to speak, two forms of time, the historical and the existential. The historical form narrates the story of Abraham's visitation by three strangers (Gen. 18:1–15), while the existential form is a revelation of the eternal God. The historical form finds its fulfilment in the existential: the worshipper is invited into the communion of love which exists between the three Persons of God. But the heart of this eternal oneness is expressed through an historical sign. The central figure, the Son, identifies himself with the sacrificial meat, while the Father's eyes and hands reach out to bless and strengthen him. The contours of their bodies run parallel: they are one; while the third angel, the Spirit, by his posture conveys this offering outward into history.

In the icon, time is not destroyed or displaced by a revelation of eternity. Further, the icon does not offer an abstract concept by which to master the relation between the two forms of time. Its message is rather that eternity is revealed in time only in the hour of Jesus Christ, as he gives himself to time out of love; conversely, that eternity can only be known in time through a personal and sacrificial movement. The way into the eternal, sacrificial heart of God faces the viewer; in the cruciform contour formed by the angels, tree and altar; in the symbol of the small, rectangular opening, to which the third angel's hand leads the eye, which is the narrow road of suffering into God's presence; and in the white table above which the angels' hands circle, which is the word of God.[7] The icon says that eternity is *now* for those willing to listen to the word, accept the cross or sit at the table of his sacrifice.

Time and the Loss of Body and Mind

The purpose of hospice care is to *give* time to living people in which to find peace and to die with dignity. At one level this means freeing time from pain's distraction; at another, it means providing patients with an environment where the cyclical and historical time on which people habitually rely is opened up and experienced as fulfilled time.

I noticed that the routine of a hospice seemed to be important for patients. They would come to know exactly when, say, the next tea round was due. It seemed to be important that time had a structure. One patient of the hospice in which I was working, whose name was Don, kept asking every few minutes what was the time. As his condition worsened he seemed to be losing his moorings in time, and he showed signs of great anxiety. These observations relate to a question, spoken or unspoken, which is asked by those diagnosed as having terminal cancer: how long have I got? Don had been told that he had nine months to live when, in fact, he rapidly deteriorated. At first both he and his wife felt angry that they had been cheated of time. If Don were to die peacefully he would have to discover in Hayward House that such time as remained had a purpose and was not just the amount of living he had left to do.

The approach of death begs the most fundamental question about the relationship between the self and time. Death is a total threat to human identity, in both its bodily and psychical aspects. We can understand this differentiation within the human psyche more clearly using symbols. Bodily identity can be represented by the figure of the mother, from whom we are born. She is the archetypal place of origin. She stands for 'the unconscious, natural and instinctive life, the physiological realm, the body in which we dwell and are contained; for the mother is also the vessel, the hollow form that carries and nourishes, and it thus stands for the foundation of consciousness'.[8] The importance of a person's body for identity should never be overlooked. As the self is the subject of a story of embodied being, so dying represents the end of self as the death of the body. It is not surprising that folk religious ideas of life after death offer little comfort to those who are facing the loss of their bodies. As Zizoulas puts it, 'The person does not simply want to be, to exist "eternally". . . . It wants something more: to exist as a *concrete*, *unique*, and *unrepeatable*, entity'.[9] The body is a guarantee of our individual reality.

On the other hand, psychical identity can be represented by the figure of the father. He is the root which every person seeks to discover to achieve stability. To have a father is to belong to a family or group with its own particular history. The father stands for the life that is gained through willing, planning and believing. He is the self we strive to become, our goal rather than our origin. This more conscious aspect of self acts in time by 'reaching out of the past and present towards anticipated goals'.[10] Death seems only to offer the goal of extinction, the end and destruction of an individual's total biography. That is why the finger of death points to the ticking clock:

> Life is first boredom, then fear.
> Whether or not we use it, it goes,
> And leaves what something hidden from us chose,
> And age, and then the only end of age.[11]

For the dying, the felt 'now' in which the self exists begins to dissolve, as there can be no 'now' which has no future or goal: 'it is not that we could ever suspend turning to new "presents", thereby suspending the flow of time; such a suspension would do away with ourselves'.[12] This aimless living, this living death is pithily captured in Beckett's tragicomedy *Waiting for Godot*:

> Vladimir: That passed the time
> Estragon: It would have passed anyway
> Vladimir: Yes, but not so quickly

So there needs to be a new beginning for the terminally ill, embracing and transcending the bodily and psychical aspects of self in the face of death. To use a modern term, the dying need to find a renewed 'psychosomatic' identity. The Fathers of the Church had a more elegant symbol. They talked of the 'heart' as the centre of all human potentiality. It was the heart that could be fulfilled, through a meeting in time with God and a sharing in his eternal life. Only in such an encounter could God's creature experience time's positive form, 'the time in which the past is fully preserved and the present is opened up to the infinity of the ages.'[13]

The Hope of New Identity

Hope, in John's Gospel, does not come in a package; it is given in personal encounter with the Word. Jesus' word finds no dwelling place in those who know who they are and who are determined not to be changed, but others hear his voice. Always his word judges the human heart. He challenges his hearers to receive a new identity as a child of God. In John 3 there is the famous dialogue between Nicodemus and Jesus. As happens so often in the Gospel a misunderstanding is used to make a theological point. Nicodemus understands the phrase 'born again' to mean a return to his mother's womb. But Jesus is saying something else. A second birth is required but not a mere repetition of the first. The second birth is the renewing of human nature 'from above',[14] which leads to *eternal life*. Every person's bodily identity must be remade by the divine wind, which blows around and about rather than being captured by the mind.

Psychical identity, too, must be remade. In John 8, Jesus radically challenges the worth of an identity based on family history. It was not the Jews' physical descent from Abraham that was disputed by Jesus (8:37) but the source of their identity, which revealed itself by their fierce adherence to the Law as their people interpreted it and by their refusal to hear Jesus' words. The issue was whether their identity should be defined by their self-made image of their forefather Abraham or by Jesus as the eternal 'I am' of God. In the course of the dialogue Jesus solemnly declares that if they find their identity in him – if they keep his word – they will *never die* (8:51).

The Gospel offers, therefore, salvation for the whole person. The Prologue makes clear the total, new identity of believers:

> But to those who did accept him
> he gave power to become children of God,
> to those who believed in his name
> who were born not from human stock
> or human desire
> or human will
> but from God himself. (1:12,13)

Believers are given a new origin from God, in the person of Jesus Christ, who is also a new goal (1:15).

This new life which has come into the world is known in community, among those who share in the divine breath (1:16f). Within community members are led into complete truth (16:7,13), that is, they taste increasingly a life of intimacy with Christ, as children of the same eternal Father. This possibility is not confined to the bounds of 'church'; the Spirit comes to all who will receive the grace and truth of Christ. In a hospice, in which suffering shakes the foundations of human identity, there is every opportunity for the eternal

Word, who became history in Jesus Christ, to address the history of patients and to lead them beyond the threat of time into the open spaces of communion, the *now*. Receiving the gift does not depend on an ability to understand doctrinal propositions, but on an act of 'letting go' of the self that seeks its own origin and goals, which we shall later call the ego, to let in new light.

I spent a long time with Albert, who while showing me old photos told me some of his memories including some of war atrocities. He himself was spared when a shell landed near him. He was close to tears as he said that he believed 'someone's looking after me'. He accepted my offer of prayer. I drew the curtains round his bed, took his hand and after a moment's silence prayed, remembering God's presence with us, giving thanks for life, love and friends, acknowledging cruelty and hate and asking for forgiveness, cleansing, peace and strength now and for evermore. Albert, who was by then crying freely, thanked me and settled down to sleep. Next time we met he thanked me again, saying, 'You'll never know the good you did me.'

The Holy Spirit met Albert in the present and freely transformed his personal identity by healing parts of his story, grounding his good and bad memories in the eternal love of God. This happened as, through prayer, he handed over his history to his Father. Albert was freed from the weight of his past to live more fully in the *now*, not simply because past memories had been healed but because hope for the future had been revealed in the present. The Holy Spirit had taken him into the communion of God which was in the beginning, bringing comfort to his restless heart. Evidence for his living in the *now* came in a marked physical and psychological recovery which was noted by the nursing staff.[15]

The journey from time to eternity is the journey from community to communion. The distance can be travelled in an instant. Finding and re-finding the way, however, requires the utmost diligence; revelation does not come down from on high in a lump but is spoken personally by Christ into history through the words and deeds of his witnesses. That is why the next chapter concerns itself with what is required of pastors who wish to be companions to the terminally ill. They must know how to be bearers of divine love, which, when bestowed by the Spirit, removes the threat of time and makes it instead the place where truth is met for eternity.

The Use of the Bible in Pastoral Care

We have already begun to use the Prologue of John's Gospel and other passages as a way of opening a window from time to eternity. These texts are not associated with pastoral care, and the use of them in this respect begs the question of the nature and authority of the Gospel, indeed, of the whole of scripture. This is the question Stephen Pattison raises again and again in his book *A Critique of Pastoral Care*. In Chapter 6, 'The Bible and Pastoral Care', he notes that 'there is an almost absolute and embarrassing silence about the Bible in pastoral care theory,'[16] and offers the first and most obvious reason for this as being that 'pastoral care is largely a product of the post-biblical church. . . The Bible is not a handbook of pastoral care'.[17] Pattison's main concern is to discourage pastors from selecting and individualising texts to bolster their authority, especially when counselling, which he feels violates the integrity of both the counselling process and the Bible. Critical scholarship has made us acutely aware that the Bible belongs to a different world from our own. Because of this, pastors 'can never fully understand the Bible or apply it for their own ends.'[18] Nonetheless, Pattison believes, there remains this place for the Bible in pastoral care:

> Pastors and those in their care are in a constant dialogue with the text of scripture, particularly liturgically. This crucially affects who they are and what they do. . . But this interaction is a *long-term, gradual* and *indirect* matter which embraces the totality of scripture in all its pluralism and not merely texts congenial to moments of intense personal need. . . The Bible's primary role in pastoral care on this understanding, then, is one of contributing to the vital task of Christian formation. This is a *background* function as far as meeting specific pastoral crises or needs is concerned.[19]

The lengthy quotation is necessary to do full justice to Pattison's position. Some may find it a satisfactory one, especially those who feel trapped by the need to be always quoting scripture in their pastoral care or those whose convictions lead them to doubt the authority of the text itself, apart from its function within community. Even so, full weight must be given to the words I have italicised. Must scripture be reduced in its authority to the level of a spiritual drip-feed or, as Pattison suggests elsewhere, to a pool of common words and images for use among the consenting faithful? There may be other ways of treating the strangeness of scripture which do the text itself more honour than this.

In the course of his analysis Pattison reviews five approaches to the Bible in pastoral care theory: the fundamentalist or biblicist; the tokenist; the imagist or suggestive approach; the informative approach; and the thematic approach. The third of these, when reviewed in the light of Pattison's criticism, will help clarify the approach taken in this book.

Alistair Campbell's work comes under scrutiny as an example of the imagist approach. Pattison acknowledges Campbell's awareness of critical method in the construction of biblical images in his book *Rediscovering Pastoral Care* (of shepherd, wounded healer and wise fool), but he criticises Campbell for not making plain his 'view of the Bible and its authority or the degree of normativeness which should be ascribed to particular scriptural texts'.[20] On the one hand, he suspects that Campbell is treating the Bible like any other great literature; on the other, he worries that he is giving to this selection of images a spurious authority because they come from the Bible. A reading of Campbell's book reveals his intention without recourse to reading between the lines. Campbell is trying to 'devise an appropriate method for discussing the nature of pastoral care – one which appeals as much to the imagination as to the intellect'.[21] So he chooses scriptural images which are suggestive and illuminating for action, ones which plumb 'the mysterious depths of human experience and its response to a living God.'[22]

If Pattison intends his own view of scripture to be consistent

he cannot object to the process of pastoral formation Campbell
is encouraging. Campbell's claim for his images is that they
have 'sufficient power'[23] to help recover the transcendent
element of pastoral care within human experience, though
'such images are only the beginning of what must be a continuing effort of the imagination.'[24] This last sentence, however, does betray a weakness inherent in 'sundering images
from the scriptural text', as Pattison puts it.[25] The danger is
that images become fodder to an imagination undisciplined by
the text from which they have sprung. Nonetheless, Pattison's
critique points to a danger rather than an insurmountable
weakness in the imagist approach.

My intention is to use some images and ideas from John's
Gospel *as they appear in the text* to point to the transcendent
foundation of pastoral care. My selection of St John's Gospel
from scripture is made first and foremost for personal reasons.
More than any other book in the Bible, it has shaped me for
the fourteen years of my conscious Christian life. The personal
nature of the choice, however, does not discount its validity:
one cannot expect the Bible as a whole to throw up its own
tidy agenda for pastoral care, and to say that a book in the
Bible has canonical status is to admit, as William Lane says,
that the text has a 'normative value. . . Canon universalizes
a text; i.e., it takes a very particular text and endows it with
a life of its own so that it may address a variety of situations
not identical with the original life situation.'[26] This authority
is in no way gainsaid by the Church's biblical scholars, who
allow us to accept both the unity and diversity of scripture
without embarrassment. Furthermore, St John's Gospel has
a lot to say about pastoral care. Its single-minded purpose is
to testify to the glory of God revealed in Jesus Christ, which
is light shining in the darkness of the world's evil, fear, ignorance and sin. It addresses the human condition in a personal
mode, offering life to the believing community. There is no
need to individualise texts from it to make them fit pastoral
situations, although there may well be a need to look at
pastoral care with fresh vision, finding a vocabulary that fits
terminal care more tightly than the general 'guiding, healing,
nurturing, reconciling and sustaining' of recent historical sum-

maries.[27] The Gospel's aim is entirely congruent with Patti-son's definition of pastoral care as 'that activity, undertaken especially by representative Christian persons, directed towards the elimination and relief of sin and sorrow and the presentation of all people perfect in Christ to God.'[28]

By adopting a textual approach, I hope to avoid the danger of divorcing images from their context. St John's Gospel is a piece of narrative theology which needs to be treated accordingly. I have therefore tried to elucidate in story-form the meaning of certain passages and then to let them rub shoulders with the story that pastor and patient will be making by their meeting. (My determination not to tie the passages down to the discussion means that they are juxtaposed into the text, without much introduction.) The 'exposition', of course, is not neutral; it reaches out to speak to a new context, but it is not squeezed ruthlessly into a foreign mould. It remains a story which resonates with the following discussion; it provokes but does not determine thought. The text's canonical authority underwrites this effort of sympathy, however much the attempt fails to do justice to the integrity of either the text or the pastoral encounter.

As for the status of the ideas and images themselves, they have the authority of witnessing to the truth. Austin Farrer, in his Brampton Lectures, *The Glass of Vision*, stated his belief that images in scripture were divinely given and had special authority, but that precisely because of this they had to be applied with the utmost care:

> Again, within the field of revealed truth, the principal images provide a canon to the lesser images. The reduction of the lesser images to terms of the greater is a theological activity. . . St John is not reducing everything to a confused simplicity. The images which he 'reduces' to terms of others no more disappear or lose their force, than do the whole body of images, when we remember that they are no more than images, and so reduce them to the one ineffable simplicity of God's saving love. All is affirmed and all is denied.[29]

The images used by St John point to Jesus Christ; in that intended function within scripture lies their authority. So, for example, the image of the shepherd applies first and foremost to Christ, the good shepherd who lays down his life for the sheep. His followers cannot be courageous without him, not by any effort of their imagination. The Bible offers images by which a pastor's imagination may be disciplined and strengthened in the purposes of saving love.

Pattison's passive model of the pastor's being gradually shaped by the text is not all there is to be said about the power of scripture. The written words bear witness to the living Word who wishes to speak truth in a new context. While there is no need for a pastor to sling texts at a patient it is essential that within the human situation a pastor should be aware of the meaning, the eternal aspect, of their meeting. A proper understanding of John's Gospel will not encourage pastors to become authoritarian, deaf to human need or trapped in a closed system of divinely sanctioned solutions; it will free them to see human vocation in a fresh way, both theirs and the patients'. It gives a burning objective to pastoral care: to let communion be formed between persons, a mutuality, through the abandoning of the autonomous self, the ego, in response to the gracious call of God in Jesus Christ. An overview of the rest of the book will make the nature of the task more apparent.

Overview

The second and third chapters cover the pastor's contribution to the building of communion. In Chapter 2, we explore the way that internal attitudes can create a climate in which there can be a deep sharing of love and disclosing of truth. Pastors cannot adopt a position apart from other members of the hospice. Like them they serve community and the needs of the terminally ill. Their faith in a God who meets humanity in the flesh, as a friend, will not allow any sense of superiority. Their authority is that of a friend who comes to witness to the unconditional love of God. Their love comprises more

than words and deeds; it has a detached quality which offers
to the terminally ill the healing that comes through awareness
of human need in the light of the presence of God. This
quality-of-being is illustrated by a meditation on the story of
the raising of Lazarus (11:1–44).

From detachment springs service, the pastoral action that
builds communion in the Holy Spirit, which is described in
Chapter 3. Service is expressed in touch and silence as much
as by word, as we shall see through a study of the washing
of the disciples' feet (13:1–30). Confrontation may be the
greatest act of service a pastor can offer, as it takes the patient
beyond his own assumptions about himself and behind
psychological defences, though the cost of doing this fruitfully
may be very great indeed. A published story from a hospital
bedside shows how the work of love pays rich dividend.

The fourth and fifth chapters are then taken up with the
response that the patient needs to make to die well. The
pastor's listening movement of silence, touch, the word of
truth, is met by a hearing response from the patient, in an
active acceptance of the love enfolding both parties to which
the pastor bears witness. Chapter 4, by a study of Jesus' claim
to be the good shepherd who lays down his life for the sheep,
demonstrates that the Passion of Christ is a victory over
suffering within pain (10:1–18). It is a human victory of obedience, available to all who respond to Love's call in the midst
of their suffering. We see it in the story of the recommissioning
of Peter (21:1–19).

Chapter 5 examines in depth the patient's work of 'letting
go', through an exposition of Jesus' saying about a single
grain of wheat falling to the ground (12:24). Here is the
answer to spiritual suffering: a willing and knowing surrender
to the call of Love. This heroic act will not be achieved
without a struggle with egocentricity, as the story of Mary of
Magdala illustrates (20:1–18). The spirit, however, comes to
the patient's aid as the presence of God within, bringing
personal meaning and hope beyond the darkness of despair.
The process fully involves the mind but is not adequately
conceived in psychological terms. The gift of eternal life,
which is knowing God, means an end to spiritual suffering,

because the heart now has, by God's grace alone, an Answer to the loss of identity which the body's decay occasions.

Chapter 6 addresses the question, 'How can a loving God judge the weak on the grounds of their faith, or lack of it?' The distinction is made between judgement and condemnation, using the story of the woman taken in adultery (7:53–8:11). Judgement happens in the decision a patient makes to accept or reject the forgiveness of Jesus Christ and the new life he offers. The pastors' place is to witness humbly and fearlessly to God's grace and truth at work in human life. Their responsibility is not to protect a patient from judgement but to offer by their care a sign of God's unconditional love, which may finally be rejected.

Chapter 7 draws together the themes of the book under the theme of glory. A meditation on Jesus' prayer of consecration (17:1–26) shows how the very humanity of Jesus makes for the glory of crucifixion. Christ's death is necessary for God to be glorified, because in dying death is defeated by an act of complete self-offering to the truth. There is universal truth to be received and revealed by the crucified. Even a death which is not painful or unjust can witness to the call of Love, in the abandoning of illusions about the nature of humanity, in the laughter of the terminally ill. Dying is a sign by which families, the hospice community and society are judged. Pastors have a small practical part to play in the spreading of glory, though their end is to find rest themselves in eternal communion.

So the book moves from a general survey of the scene to considering each partner of the meeting in turn, and then moves back to the generality to complete a revolution in the circle of seeing. Anyone who reads John's Gospel cannot fail to notice how certain basic themes appear again and again in different guises. If the pattern of this book is congruent with that pattern the author will be well pleased.

2

MAKING SPACE FOR MEETING –
PASTORAL ATTITUDES

True life is found in communion with Christ, in the eternal realm. This was the conclusion of the first part of Chapter 1. The question presses, then, of how communion can be enabled in practice. The theme of this book is not so much patients' needs and how they may be tended but the grace of God's truth and how it is revealed to all who seek it. So while this chapter and the next never lose sight of the needs of the dying, they dwell on the issue of pastoral identity, for it is pastors whose vocation it is to offer to others in word, deed, and in their very being, God's true life. A patient's needs do come before a pastor's, but the patient must not be subjected to a caring undisciplined by love. The pastor has to know how to facilitate a relationship in which love can be shared and truth disclosed. These next two chapters try to assist the journey from community to communion by talking about attitudes and actions which do enable the growth of mutuality between persons. It sets the stage for the discovery of personal hope beyond suffering, which Chapters 4 and 5 will consider.

We begin by setting the pastoral task within community. The hospice, with or without a pastor, offers a home for the dying. So the pastor must find a place which is at once her own but which also allows her to belong to the whole in a distinct way. Faith cannot be an item which causes the pastor to stand aloof nor one which blurs the reality of suffering; it must make for living community. The pastor's particular identity is one of friend and servant to the dying. She offers herself to the dying as an equal among experts, realising a common humanity, a common vulnerability in the face of suffering. Yet her awareness of God allows her to deal in human darkness without fear and to make room there for God to act. These attitudes are essential for good pastoral care and open the way to a true meeting of persons.

The emphasis in the next chapter shifts from necessary pastoral attitudes to pastoral acts enabling the growth of communion. The pastor serves her friends with a detached love, which is founded on the vision of God and which harnesses the power of silence, touch and prayer. She and all those who love and affirm the dying person will encourage him to receive his body as a gift and not to cling to it as a possession. The pastor's calling is to dwell with the patient, listening to him and to God for the word of truth which brings life. But in this chapter we start with the central question of how a pastor fits into the hospice community.

Community and Faith

W.H. Vanstone identifies three, related factors which form the basis of true community; stability, sense of identity and cause.[1] *Stability* is ensured by the commitment of staff to work with each other for the common good, and to maintain lines of communication, even when personalities and styles of working clash. A hospice, while sharing the medical, nursing and administrative functions of a hospital, has a distinct *identity* as a home for the terminally ill. All members of the hospice family have their eyes set on patients' needs; all staff, no matter what their role, would see themselves as carers, helpers and supporters. They have chosen to work with those who are dying. Their *cause* is the valuing of whole persons in the face of death, which means caring not just for an individual but also with and for other family members and friends. These three factors, running together, make the hospice a place where residents are enabled to live until they die in safety, rather than a place for people to come to wait for death.

The pastor is no more important a figure in the hospice than any other person whom God has given the patient in his total human need. The one who serves the tea and has time for a natter can give as much as the specialist. Unblocking a patient's bowels is often far more necessary than talking about God. Community leaves no room for a self-righteous individual who fights for a secret cause. Anyone who wants to pastor has to find a place within the hospice team and, in a distinct way, to embody the whole ministry of the community. It is commonplace to talk of pastors as people of faith. Yet faith is not a commodity which can be exchanged in a barter of propositions nor is it a cheap antidote to despair. There is no place for pastoring 'from above' in the manner of Charles Causley's second type of hospital visitor, who appears,

> . . . a melancholy splurge
> Of theological colours;
> Taps heavily about like a healthy vulture
> Distributing deep-frozen hope.[2]

Faith, also, must serve the human needs of the dying person. It comes from community and is meant for community.

John's Gospel may not immediately appear to be a well from which a suitable spirituality can be drawn. Professor James Dunn says that 'John's concept of worship is individualistic . . . John thinks in terms of the individualism of direct inspiration and relationship – that is, not independent of other believers, but not dependent on them either'.[3] But this is a misrepresentation of John's purpose, which was to root the Christian *community* deeper in faith.[4] Faith for John is not exhausted in the acceptance of fact or doctrine,[5] neither is it essentially an existential commitment expressed in and through doctrine.[6] In John's Gospel, faith is most closely related to love, and love to knowledge. The latter connection is firmly established in verse 18 of the Prologue, where the Word of God is identified with the Son of God. Only the uniquely loved Son of God can reveal the Father faithfully. He comes from the Father's bosom and speaks directly out of his knowledge of the Father and the Father's knowledge of him.

Faith, love, knowledge – all these are modelled for

community in Jesus' relationship with his Father and worked out in personal dialogue with different types through the Gospel story. The Word brings a word (5:24, 15:3), a revelation which is 'not so much a divine idea but a divine communication'.[7] He does not stay aloof from the material world but is made flesh to reveal in our history the eternal communion of love which sustains creation. The Father gives his Son to the world to communicate light, life and love to his creatures. The source of these gifts is the revelation of the knowledge of the truth which Jesus gives to his disciples in personal encounter, which makes for a community of faith.

In John 4, Christ initiates an astonishing human encounter across barriers of sexual, racial and religious prejudice (v. 27). He shares a common thirst with a Samaritan woman at a well. Through her questioning of and argument with him, Jesus reveals himself as Messiah. At the level of doctrine her faith hardly exists: can this perhaps be the Christ (v. 29)?[8] Yet John approves of her hesitant response to Jesus, which is really focussed much more on his knowledge of her than on hers of him.[9] The woman's response, however, takes her back to her community, where the excitement of her being known as a person becomes an invitation to others to make their own pilgrimage to Christ. The coming of Jesus, therefore, allows more than new relationship with God. Through him the possibility exists of new community, through the defeat of egocentricity.

The truth offered by Jesus is universal. He brings light and life to 'that which was his own' (1:11). This revelation is given to the world, however, at the level at which it most needs to be received, the personal. The gospel offers to every person true love for self and for God, which can only be based on knowledge of the truth. Faith is a growing into the truth, given in an encounter with the risen Christ through the gift of the Spirit, who is the Spirit of truth (14:17, 15:26, 16:13). While John does not spell out the social implications of 'dwelling in Christ' that does not mean to say that he imagines a community vaguely bound by a common sense of individual inspiration. As we shall see in the next chapter, where disciples love one another as Christ has loved them, community takes on the special depth and shape of human communion.

Human Need and Pastoral Identity

Pastors are present in a hospice to share in its community life and to extend it by the gift of their faithful presence at the side of patients. Their calling is to found a relationship which is based on a proper understanding of faith. Faith is not a religious commodity but the way by which truth may be found within human existence. This is important because patients of the hospice are vulnerable and cannot stand being treated as conversion fodder. They are defenceless and have often to hand themselves over to the experts.[10] They are having to learn a new way of living as those who are, at best, cared for and, at worst, acted on.

RR: *You've just been to the toilet, Don.*
Don: *Oh yes, sorry. Aren't I allowed to go?*
RR: *No, of course you're allowed to go. It's just that you went a few moments ago.*
Don: *Sorry, Doctor.*

Those who are involved with hospice care speak with one voice about the pastoral needs of a dying person. A patient should be enabled to perceive and affirm meaning for their life through a caring, supportive and unambiguous relationship which promotes trust and affirms human worth and dignity. 'The helper's role is of a listener – clarifying, supporting, exploring, reflecting. The helper/client relationship is between equals'.[11] Edgar Jackson stresses how necessary for effective communication is a desire for real encounter with the dying. He also points to the need to create basic trust and the ability to listen for hidden meanings.[12] For Kübler-Ross the most important quality is to be ready and willing to share the patient's concerns.[13] All these people are talking the language of intimate human encounter and loving companionship centred on the patient.

While pastors share in the stability of the hospice and share its aim of serving the needs of the dying, the main difference between them and other members of the community lies in their sense of identity. The hospice movement certainly does not exclude spiritual dimensions in terminal care; doctors, nurses and ancillary staff may all find themselves exchanging their usual role for a pastoral one; but a pastor's sights are set primarily at the spiritual level. Pastors come from the community of faith to offer community to the world. Their cause is the breaking down of egocentricity between persons, so that tragedy becomes an opportunity for grace. They attempt to offer the stability of unconditional love: God's love could not be truly free unless it were unconditional, otherwise it could not be offered without the knowledge that it would be reciprocated. They come as a friend and servant, to share another's darkness and, protected and empowered within the darkness by knowledge of God, to witness to the Light.

To be a friend and servant of the vulnerable means that pastors have to be able to deal in darkness. If a pastor thinks of herself as set apart to preach a gospel of doctrinal propositions which, however simple, must be accepted before God will enter a person's life, then a patient cannot be accepted as an equal by that pastor until and unless he shows evidence of having accepted these propositions. The pastor stands apart from the patient as *the one who knows* (the truth; the eternal future of the dying person – either 'heaven' or 'hell'; the stage theory of dying) or as *the one who gives* (service, hope, time). She may also feel herself to be, by virtue of escaping many encounters with death and dying, *the one who lives for ever*. Truly this pastor is a god: holy, strong and immortal! She is not, however, one who shares human grief and carries sorrow as a friend.

W.B. Yeats' poem 'Crazy Jane meets the Bishop' [14] tells of an encounter between a haughty bishop and a 'fool' who, in the romantic tradition, speaks the truth about holiness and pride.

> A woman can be proud and stiff
> When on love intent;
> But Love has pitched his mansion in
> The place of excrement; [15]
> For nothing can be sole or whole
> That has not been rent.

Brokenness is an essential part of pastoral ministry because it is an essential part of friendship with broken people. John's Gospel points the pastor firmly to a Christ who meets humanity by becoming broken: 'the Word became *flesh*' says that God has become one with us in our poverty, sharing human weakness and mortality. The Word became flesh for our sake, through an astonishing act of condescension and self-abnegating love, coming down as man for us to save us as man.[16] As I have said, the patient is already vulnerable and cannot be proud in the weakness of his flesh; but the pastor must also recognise her own weakness and mortality.

Fear can hold a pastor back from friendship: fear of losing control or respect; fear of being hurt too deeply by death; and fear of feeling, or of being, helpless.[17] But the pastor's humanity is held as firmly in Christ's friendship as is the patient's. She is free to abandon the place of pride and certainty – among 'the Jews' in Johannine terms – and to trust Jesus to reveal himself in personal encounter. Because Christ, by his Spirit, is already unconditionally present in the encounter, it is unnecessary to attempt to force Christ into the situation through the exchange of propositions.[18] The pastor does know Jesus and, if the patient is not a Christian, she may discern his presence more clearly than does the patient. Yet both are set to learn something new of the God who 'shared the dirt and the sweat, the bafflement and loneliness, the pain, the weakness, yes, and the death too . . . [One who] did it all as one of us'.[19] The pastor can be vulnerable because God in Christ has made himself vulnerable to the world's sorrow.[20]

There is more to good pastoral care than being vulnerable to human suffering in friendship. Christ did not, even in friendship, react to the suffering of others on a merely emotional level. Christ brought his serenity to bear upon human suffering wherever he met it, in others or in himself; on the cross, he took even the suffering of painful dying into his eternal relationship with God, in an act of loving obedience. His words, too, brought life, precisely because they were not as others', but full of grace and truth. In John 15, deeds and words are joined under the theme of friendship. There can be no greater love than freely laying down one's life for a friend. Jesus first does this for his own friends, revealing on the cross the full depth of his friendship with God and humanity. The words he speaks out of his love for the Father he shares out of friendship for the disciples, to win their friendship. Their obedience, to be worked out in their friendship with one another, is a fruit and sign of the friendship which Jesus has initiated with his disciples, as well as with his Father.

Beyond deed and word even, there is a depth of friendship which can only be called a quality-of-being in the world, a detachment. We are shown this in John 11 where Christ is confronted by the needs, real and apparent, of his friends. This story of the raising of Lazarus contains the truth of Christ being the resurrection for all who believe in him. The reader is pointed beyond the tensions of the plot to the stature of its chief actor. So we can draw out Christ's majestic bearing from the story to provoke insight into the nature and place of detachment in pastoral care.

Detachment, a Sign of Friendship

A simple request is delivered to Jesus from his followers Mary and Martha: 'Lord, the man you love is ill.' You should know this because if you were here you could heal him. From the outset there are pressures on Jesus to react quickly, in a human fashion, to fulfil the healing role his friends hope of him. Instead, Jesus responds to the knowledge of his own deepest calling to bring life: 'This sickness will not end in death, but it is for God's glory so that through it the Son of God may be glorified.' Already, he knows that Lazarus will 'rest', though death will not have the last word. Rather than by a healing, God will be given glory in the sign of Lazarus' raising, and through it his Son will be glorified; that is, the raising will take Christ into his passion. Jesus knows both the value and the cost of this sign. Already, when there seems no danger in going to Lazarus, Christ can foresee what will happen, and this knowledge, not the pressing demands of human emotion, determines Jesus' action: 'Jesus loved Martha and her sister and Lazarus, yet when he heard that he was ill he stayed where he was for two more days.' He stays so that his going will be the more fruitful for his friends and the cost to him not be too small.

After Lazarus has died the time is right for Christ to lead his disciples into danger. He knows that he must go to face death squarely, to show that, in God's power, it is a sleep from which the faithful can be awoken. Only by embracing death can death be overcome. His disciples, however, do not travel by such inner light. They are afraid because, as yet, they see only naturally, in the world's light. Thomas says to the others, 'Let us also go to die with him', but this is a fatalistic counsel of a blind man, someone who can see neither God's protection in the present nor the miracle to come nor, finally, the freely accepted passion required of Christ and of any disciple to overcome death.

Mary and Martha have passed beyond the point of fear. Death having visited them, they have nothing left for fear to defend. Both meet him with the reproachful plea, 'Lord, if you had been here my brother would not have died.' Yet Jesus' perspective remains unique. Despite the mounting wave of grief which comes to a crest in Mary flinging herself at Jesus' feet weeping, he speaks and acts with a complete authority which is at once compassionate, gentle and true. He invites Martha to believe beyond the bounds of reason or religious faith by pointing her to his deepest identity for her as Resurrection, now and not at the last day, which he is revealing by not having healed her brother: 'I am the resurrection and the life. Anyone who believes in me, even though that person dies, will live, and whoever lives and believes in me will never die. Do you believe this?'

To Martha, Jesus gives a word of resurrection; the sign follows the arrival of Mary and those attending her. He is profoundly moved by Mary's tears and those of the mourners around; but he does not catch tears from them. Christ grieves at what he knows. In him God's own love is expressed and experienced humanly. From the awareness of his mortality he reaches out with divine compassion to those he has been sent by the Father to save. It is the grief of one who sees ignorance, sorrow and death as an affront to the glory of God and the reality of his coming. Jesus, having passed through indignation and distress, begins to weep for Lazarus, for Mary and Martha, for the Jews and for the whole world. He could indeed, as some wondered, have done something earlier to prevent Lazarus from dying, but at the expense of hiding salvation from the world; now he does what he must as the Resurrection do: 'Where have you put him?' he asks those who can see nothing but their grief, and his.

So Jesus is taken to the place of death with a vision of the glory of God about to be revealed. He is not spared human feeling through detachment. Quite the contrary: his human feeling is intensified in the face of the darkness he must wrestle with for the Father's sake. All this weight and breadth of sorrow, however, possesses a dynamism as intercession, as the weeping Jesus makes his way into his Father's presence. It is offered to the Father for his dealing. Jesus is always praying, but at this point, for the sake of those who do not yet believe, he reveals his inner life, opening the window onto a relationship of mutual hearing. Jesus publicly stands apart before he acts. Out of his prayer comes an end to his own super-human grief in a cry which shakes the roots of death: 'Lazarus, come out!' His grieving is magnificently fruitful, the seedbed of the Word of life to Lazarus, and a revelation of the vulnerability of the One who defeats ignorance, sorrow and even death by the power of a life lived looking to the Father.

Not a Role but a Way of Being

The drama of the story of Lazarus' raising is heightened by the majesty of Jesus. Those who look on can penetrate neither the meaning of his words nor of his tears. He has to explain and enact who he is for them. He himself, however, knows who he is, and it is this self-knowledge that always guides him, first holding him back from his friends, then sending him towards his enemies. His self-awareness in no way obscures his feelings but informs them; they, in turn, humanise all that he does as Word to bring life to his friends. Christ does not come to stage a miracle, but to reveal his true identity. Having no role to play, he is free from every expectation placed upon him. His whole being is concentrated on the mission he has been given, which will remake human hope by destroying all lesser hopes. His detachment is totally at one with his purpose to save; without it, salvation would not be possible.

Describing Christ's attitude in this story as one of 'detachment' in no way implies that he is indifferent to suffering or that his love is not genuine. William Vanstone rejects detachment as a mark of 'authentic' love because he defines it as a 'self-sufficiency unaffected and unimpaired in the one who professes to love'.[21] Detachment as Jesus practises it, however, is not self-sufficiency: it is the human side of an intense relationship with God. Detachment need not mean 'a closing-off of the "affective", feeling parts of our humanness', as Rowan Williams describes the popular suspicion; as he says, it might be the way in which 'we form our affective life into something distinctively human – something reflective and imaginative, something about which we can think and hope, not simply something that happens to us, a fate, an accident.'[22] Furthermore it might be, as it was for Jesus, the way in which feelings are raised into the eternal realm through prayer.

Because theologians of repute suspect detachment,[23] it is vital to define its meaning carefully. Detachment is certainly not the same thing as neat professionalism. Wesley Carr comes perilously close to this position as he attempts to help pastors resist the 'seduction' of incarnational ministry, that is, the temptation to think of 'being with' those in need as an end in itself. A desire to achieve oneness with others at all costs, he says, causes pastors to produce 'vacuous and impotent responses',[24] as they smother creative differences and smooth over awkward feelings such as hostility or dislike. Their calling, however, is not 'merely to be, but by being and believing to achieve'.[25] Carr's solution to the problem of pastoral ineffectiveness is 'to become less aware of ourselves as persons and more alert to our roles ... *Who* we are as persons does matter, but for the pastoral ministry in human relationship we need a strong sense of *what* we are, our role'. The emphasis, established for Christians by the model of the incarnation, is always first upon role and second upon person, because in our assigned roles lies our vulnerability'.[26]

Carr's model of the incarnation does not square with the words of John's Gospel. We have seen that Jesus did not deal with people on the basis of the roles they offered him but from the foundation of who he was, what we may call his 'I am'. Those who are terminally ill are quick to sense a 'professional' approach, and this is indeed the flavour that Carr's words convey. For him, feelings are a tool a pastor uses to inform her inward self of how her outward persona is managing a client's expectations. His hope is that 'a creative working relationship, leads to discovery for all involved — growth or conversion'.[27] This language, in both tone and content, suggests an engagement that works from the skin inward to a satisfactory and beneficial depth. Separating person from role and then giving role a priority cannot prepare us for a real meeting between persons.

Carr is right to acknowledge the dangers of over-identification with a patient. William May, writing about professional medical care, says, 'It will not do to pretend to be the second person of the Trinity, prepared to make with every patient the sympathetic descent into his suffering. . . It is important to remain emotionally free so as to be able to withdraw the self when [one's] services are no longer pertinent.'[28] While it is true that there are important differences between the professional detachment of a medic and the bearing of a pastor, it is interesting to note that May's emphasis falls on retaining the freedom to withdraw the self from suffering, not just a body of expertise from a condition. So, too, pastors must avoid the patronising attitude,[29] whether expressed verbally or not, which says, 'I know how you feel'. Yet it is possible to defend the uniqueness of each person's suffering while at the same time not dismissing the idea of 'being with' people in their need. This is the case Alistair Campbell advances in his seminal book, *Rediscovering Pastoral Care*.

Awareness and Transcendence

Campbell believes that a pastor can mediate healing because 'he or she is able to convey, as much by presence as the words used, both an awareness and a transcendence of loss.'[30] We have so far defined detachment in mainly negative terms: detachment prevents over-identification, but is neither indifference nor aloofness. Campbell's perspective can help us towards a positive definition of detachment as a quality-of-being. The transcendence of Jesus revealed in the gospel finds resonance in Campell's emphasis on the neglected, transcendent element of pastoral care, which he talks about in terms of integrity.[31] His understanding of caring forces the pastor to reconsider his inner resources: 'we also lack courage in action and in words, mainly because there is no sure centre to our being.'[32] For pastors to achieve anything they must, as Jesus did, act and speak from their own 'I am'.

In contrast to Carr, Campbell finds the true location of vulnerability not in our roles but in our wounds. Though we try to avoid being wounded, when we meet wounds we find them to be a source of communion; they become 'openings in our bodily walls'.[33] Recognition of a common human condition forms the bedrock for human encounter, though only healed wounds can bring healing to others. For Campbell, the stuff of the encounter is the very depths of personal being. No neat boundaries exist to confine what is possible. As he says, 'We can only share in someone else's life search if we are prepared to expose ourselves a little, speaking about things which matter deeply to us as well as the other and risking ourselves in service of the other.'[34] The qualifying phrase 'a little' is not meant to protect the pastor from risk but the patient from being overwhelmed by a weight of passion which denies freedom. The pastor humbly offers her whole self as a resource for the other.

Campbell's understanding of pastoral care is, in many ways, as strongly mediated as is Carr's model by roles. The mediating agency here, though, is self-knowledge, an awareness which Anthony de Mello takes as the organising principle of his spiritual writing:

Even though it was the Master's day of Silence, a travel-
ler begged for a word of wisdom that would guide him
through life's journey.
The Master nodded affably, took a sheet of paper and
wrote a single word on it: 'Awareness.'
The visitor was perplexed. 'That's too brief. Would you
please expand on it a bit?'
The Master took the paper back and wrote: 'Awareness,
awareness, awareness.'
'But what do these words *mean*?' said the stranger helplessly.
The Master reached out for the paper and wrote: 'Awareness, awareness, awareness means *awareness*.'[35]

A story like this characterises well the nature of detachment.
It cannot be reduced to concepts. It is a transcendent quality
which reflects the divine life itself found among those who
have been saved from the power of sin and death by the grace
of God. An aware person has something to communicate to
others from the depths of her being which, though beyond
definition, may also be called salvation. Douglas Davies is
right to see the experience of salvation as a 'dynamic element'
that forms identity, as 'a form of super-identity'.[36] Only an
aware person will confer healing through her humble service
to others. She is someone with a history of being loved and a
knowledge of her own nothingness without God. Her being is
proof of Jesus' words, 'I am the vine, you are the branches.
Whoever remains in me, with me in him, bears fruit in plenty;
for cut off from me you can do nothing' (15:5).

In awareness, emotions are not lost, but they are stripped
of their compulsive quality. As de Mello says, 'you keep your
softness, your subtleness, your gentleness, your openness, your
flexibility, and you don't push, change occurs'.[37] Instead of
driving an individual to react unreflectively, emotion is taken
into prayerfulness. Jesus Christ was not bound to what early
tradition called passions; he lived in a state of complete surrender to his Father. Notably similar stories to the beginning
of John 11 are preserved in the Desert Fathers, where a monk

resists the temptation to leave his cell to visit a sick brother because to venture out would be to respond to passion and so to act unfruitfully. Conversely, a freedom from being driven is a freedom to pray, to allow passions to be educated into true feeling.

It is difficult to gain awareness in suffering, especially where religious culture exalts activism and therapeutic technique. But the goal is worth pursuing, for what is offered is 'the wound of knowledge'.[38] Far from being rendered indifferent to suffering, a praying person will become sensitised to it. For example, a Sister involved in hospice work wrote, 'After the funeral there was nothing left to do but to be there beside her. Surrounded by grief too immense for words I felt physical pain which still recurs from time to time when I least expect it. By staying alongside I was absorbing a little of her pain.'[39] Awareness allows an engagement with the reality of human suffering in which feeling finds fulfilment in personal surrender to the saving purposes of God. This way of meeting suffering prayerfully not only protects the pastor from inner compulsion, from attempting to soothe her own festering wounds in another's blood, but also frees her from any external demand made on her by the patient. Detachment, therefore, is a necessary and proper defence against illegitimate or unnecessary exhaustion, and enables the pastor to find the resources to act within the situation, as Campbell would put it, with 'integrity'. It frees her to give out of unconditional love.

Awareness means, above everything, that one *sees* before one *does* anything. In an environment where a patient is often being acted upon rather than being dwelt with, a pastor has a crucial non-role to play, as friend. Because she has no earnest, professional endeavour to perform, she will be free to laugh at her own impotence and at the ridiculous human condition. Nevertheless, knowing her helplessness, this friend will speak and act fruitfully, because she will be listening with a trusting heart: God stands between her and another, as a bridge to reality and a defence from romanticism; only in and through him can true love flow. 'Being with' another is not so vacuous a response if the result is a union of love which transcends bodily boundaries. As Temple Gairdner wrote as he looked forward to his marriage,

> That I may come near to her,
> draw me nearer to you than to her;
> that I may know her,
> make me to know you more than her;
> that I may love her
> with the love of a perfectly whole heart
> cause me to love you more than her and most of all.[40]

3

BUILDING COMMUNION –
PASTORAL ACTS

A firm pastoral identity promotes good attitudes which will certainly bear fruit in acts of love. This is the line of thought we are following. Loving friendship which is aware both of God's will and human need will express itself in acts of service. Silence, touch and speech can all serve the transfiguration of community into communion. When used with awareness each is part of one language of love. Speech has a particular role to play in helping a patient see the truth of life, and this sometimes involves confrontation. When this is done without aggression, however, these moments are often the ones through which hope springs eternal, as old assumptions are overturned and defences abandoned. The cost of creating a community of trust in which it is possible to face the truth is enormous. The chapter ends with some practical examples of service and its impact on terminal care.

In John 13, we witness the power that awareness brings to action, even as darkness closes round. As the hour of his Passion begins, Jesus gives a sign under which every act and word which follow it must be interpreted. The knowledge that he must leave the world and those given to him to protect in it by his own Father draws from him a work of extreme poignancy. The devil is abroad, seeking to bring about Jesus' betrayal, but nothing can prevent Jesus from fulfilling the mission that his Father has entrusted to him, for the Father whom he knows as a Son and who empowers him is none other than God himself.

Service, Friendship in Action

When supper is over, Jesus, fully aware of his Father's will, rises from table, removes his outer garments and, having taken a towel, ties it round his waist. Quite without warning, the disciples' Lord and Master has become their slave. Jesus' deliberate act foreshadows his exaltation on the cross, not any humiliation. Jesus cannot be humiliated because his life is devoid of pride. The only life he knows is the one he lives in all its fullness through obedience to the One who sent him. So he faces his hour of death with the immense inner authority of a man who knows where he comes from and what is his destiny. The washing of the disciples' feet is the act of someone totally aware of his own dependence on the Father and of the call to drink his cup of suffering. Christ is, to the core of his being, a servant of the will of God.

In serving his disciples in this way, Jesus reveals with a fresh urgency the uttermost love the Father has for the Son and wishes to reveal in the world through the Son. His washing, which so startles those who follow him, gathers up in a single act all that has been hidden to them and all that they will later understand, because it confers the self-giving love of the Father. Jesus, the servant of God's love, lays down his life freely, choosing as his instruments a towel and a pitcher, as later, to serve his own, he will carry his cross. The water is poured out into a basin for his disciples, as later, it will flow from his side into the world. By loving his disciples just as the Father has loved him Jesus fulfils the purpose of his coming, which is 'to bring near to men the distant and strange, unfamiliar and misunderstood God.'[1] The God he reveals is a Father who is given to serving his creatures and in serving reveals their need to be cleansed.

No word is needed to explain the extremity of this bodily act; rather, in silence the act gathers its power. Peter breaks the dramatic tension with words. As Jesus approaches him he asks, horrified, 'Lord, are you going to wash my feet?' Though he does want to be close to Jesus, Peter finds it next to impossible to receive this service. Now a word is needed, to prevent Peter rejecting the whole meaning of Jesus' ministry:

'At the moment you do not know what I am doing, but later you will understand.' This gives no reassurance to Peter. He is sure of the proper respect due to his Lord: 'Never! You shall never wash my feet!' 'If I do not wash you, you can have no share with me,' replies Jesus in truth. The Father has put everything into his hands and from his hands his own must receive everything. They must not draw back from his complete self-giving because of anything they themselves think they can or should offer. They must discover their dependence on the love of the Son, however much the truth humbles them. Peter must allow himself to be cleansed by receiving Jesus' word to him. And if Peter cannot understand it for now, at least he must accept the outward sign; otherwise, like Judas, he will be rejecting the saving love which is carried by it.

Jesus' example challenges every conception of what it means to belong to his community. Before the washing, the disciples shared table fellowship, bound together by their common allegiance to their host and Master. Now Jesus sits down among them to explain that the depth of their love for each other should match his for them. If they cannot let pride come between themselves and God, so also they cannot let it come between each other. They ought to love one another practically, serving each other with the same humility as their Lord has just shown. But the washing not only challenges the disciples; it has also changed them. When Jesus resumes his place at table, he is speaking to those who have been purified through receiving his ministry. He does not expect any of his own to follow his example before they have met love in the flesh: 'If I, then, the Lord and Master, have washed your feet,' says Jesus, 'you must wash each other's feet.' Jesus leaves his disciples with a pattern of love into which they have been taken by his washing. His saving action has planted the seed of true sonship in their hearts.

The disciples' service can only be secured once Jesus has finished his own service to them by giving up the living water of the Spirit. The love which presses in on the disciples and demands the abandoning of their former conception of their God, themselves and their friends is the same love which will take Jesus to the cross. Jesus must love them to the end, putting himself at the entire disposal of his own, his body meeting their bodily needs, because only by receiving the Spirit from his hands will they, in turn, be able to hand on what they have received. In the Spirit their service will flow freely from their Master's love, just as Jesus' service flowed from his Master's. The cross will finally seal this pattern of love in history. Its victory will be to put within reach a life of sonship, where those who drink of the Spirit will find that they too can love, even to the end.

Silence and Touch in the Service of Community

Jesus' washing of the disciples' feet reveals how necessary a foundation of silence is for the making of true community. There is inner silence – Jesus' knowing of the hour, his knowledge of his Father's will and his friends' need (13:1,3) – a silence of awareness, from which the silent action of loving service flows, which is the silence of pure gift (13:4,5). The word then spoken out of silence confronts Peter exactly at his point of need, knowing challenging unknowing, and humility pride. Where community might have broken down, it takes instead a decisive step forward in trust. Once the washing has been received and the disciples taken into Christ's silence they are ready to hear his new commandment, that they should love one another. The truth stands on silence. Pastors who wish to follow Christ, then, can take no short cut to service. Before they are in a position to love others as Christ has loved them, they themselves must be loved: they must receive Christ's service silently, going through the same painful washing as Peter had to face. If they have not been humbled by being served as they truly are, with dirt between their toes, and if they have not had to surrender to the will of Christ in a bodily, that is, in a completely human, way, they can be of no service to others. When words of self-justification cease, when need is admitted, when cleansing is received and its wonder known, then disciples have something to offer community-making.

The influence of secular theory has given rise to the expectation that the best preparation for service is to learn, mainly verbal, techniques of counselling.[2] It should be no surprise, however, to think of silence as the best preparation for ministry. The whole tradition of contemplative action in the church points to the need to renounce self and let God use people otherwise useless to him in his service.[3] T.S. Eliot points to this necessity in the second of his Four Quartets:

> I said to my soul, be still, and wait without hope
> For hope would be hope for the wrong thing; wait
>   without love
> For love would be love of the wrong thing; there is yet
>   faith.
> But the faith and the love and the hope are all in the
>   waiting.
> Wait without thought for you are not ready for thought:
> So the darkness shall be light, and the stillness the
>   dancing.[4]

A person who is not afraid to wait in darkness before God will be more able to avoid erecting defences against the pain of another's darkness or the stench of another's physical decay; she will not succumb to parentalism, an infrangible cheerfulness, the tendency to chatter or an over-keenness to perform religious rites on the patient, such as praying, reading scripture or bringing holy communion. Her fearlessness will provide an atmosphere in which the patient will feel able to abandon some of his own defences, and her humility will open their meeting to truth.

Silence serves community because it bears the message that a dying person does not have a problem which needs solving by a superior. The silent person need not produce pat answers, especially to the cry 'Why me?'; she comes as companion, carrying an Answer in her own heart which can only be communicated through an intense vigilance.[5] The pastor's trust is not in words but in a God who wishes to speak through us. Sometimes the Word will come through words, other times a patient will hear the Word 'from the look on another's face or catch the sound of it in his heart – in a heart that lives, that radiates life and awakens life.'[6] As we have seen in John 13, silence enhances the value of both word and deed. We shall come to the business of speaking presently, but here must be mentioned the language of touch, the way in which being present-in-love is expressed bodily.

As it is in the Gospel story, touch is part of a much wider language of signs. It is not simply that a dying person is touched – there are many occasions when this happens routinely – but that touch is unsolicited and applied with utmost awareness of human need. Sometimes it will be right to hold a hand, sometimes to stroke or caress, sometimes to put an arm around a shoulder, sometimes to kiss. Detachment helps the pastor to discern what sort of touch feels comfortable in the meeting. In general, men find it harder both to give and receive touch,[7] but most patients will come to a point when they want to be touched because it says, 'You are not alone: whatever happens, I am with you'. This of course is to speak metaphorically. Touch need not be sustained to convey this message; the memory of being touched lingers in the heart, allowing a pastor to use touch to take leave gracefully as well as to make stay. Sometimes touch even says to a body who refuses loving concern, 'I shall accept your rejecting me: I'll serve you by not being here.' As in the Gospel, signs need not be received.

Touch has two basic functions. First, it communicates certain physical information that gives an indication of mental and emotional states. A hand may grip, squeeze or rest in another's. From the hand one can sense changes in heartbeat and body temperature. The patient, too, can feel the response of a friend through touch. When the patient is in a state of chronic or acute confusion, touch becomes vital for the maintenance of a sense of personal identity.[8] Second, touch is a way into communion. As Autton says, 'Once we have entered into communion with the dying through touch we begin to love them much more than we could ever have loved them in life.'[9] Touch, when used sensitively, will become a fleshly channel of grace. As silence can enhance the value of touch, so touch can take both parties into silence. When we are 'in touch' there is no need to force a connection between persons with words. Touching enables human hearts to meet because it affirms the whole mystery of embodiment in the face of death.

As a sign, touch carries like power to Jesus' washing of the disciples' feet (and may be rejected as violently by those who most need it): those who touch with awareness draw others into real, bodily communion. Knowing themselves as servants, they convey the eternal self-giving love of the Father. Only bodily love can affirm and maintain the uniqueness of the person. The body is not only important for the reason that it holds a patient's biography but also, and maybe more significantly, because it is the body which has been loved by others as the concrete self.[10] Indeed, the self has been shaped by the body-loving of others.[11] Yet loving touch, while affirming identity, does not encourage a person to hang on desperately to the body. It reveals that 'one is loved for what one is, which allows one to accept oneself and to receive one's own being as a gift'.[12] The body is precious, yes, but it is a precious *gift* and not a precious *possession*.

The communion which touch creates takes both parties into the realm of grace. If the body is felt as gift then beyond and within human loving there may be a giver. The friendship that says we are not on our own invites the conclusion that we are not our own. As Evdokimov says, 'the voice of grace is never that of a tyrant; it is an invitation, a call from the Friend. I accept it for today in the contours of my present situation until the moment when I will *perhaps* see more clearly'.[13] Words can help in this revelation, interpreting bodily action, so that, as in John's Gospel, 'the historical event becomes a sign of an invisible reality which it reveals'.[14] But if touch is a sign needing interpretation, so also touch allows the necessary words to be spoken with detachment: they cease to be aimed across a gap between individuals and become a shared exploration of the mystery of enfolding Love.

Speaking the Truth in Love

Our discussion has already shown the difficulty of separating silence, touch and word. Talking of silence as listening has allowed us to understand it as a medium from which speech and action flow. It would be just as right, though, to describe silence as a peace in which speech and action find their rest. So as we start to discuss speaking the truth, we cannot leave behind talk of silence. Touch, silence and speaking are part of one language of love; without having a home in silence, words cannot create communion. As Alistair Campbell says, 'Words are often the enemy of care, for they seduce the carer and the cared for into playing verbal games, concealing still further the wholeness they might be able to seek together, if they did not fear the simplicity of silence'.[15] On the other hand, words there must be: silence has many negative meanings,[16] and it is equally true to say that silence can only create communion when the right words are spoken, ones assuring the patient that he is accepted as he is.

The Prologue of John's Gospel gives a good insight into the dialectic between word and silence. The Word's speaking issues from his being with the Father, while also through speaking the Word's being with the Father is maintained. In the Incarnation, we see this reality revealed in a human life. Christ's words flow from the eternal and inner silence of relationship, while also he speaks because he must stay obedient to the Father:

> For I have not spoken of my own accord;
> but the Father who sent me
> commanded me what to say and what to speak,
> and I know that his commands mean eternal life.
> And therefore what the Father has told me
> is what I speak. (12:49f)

Like Jesus, a pastor must speak what she is given to say, so that words witness to their source in God rather than contributing to a rootless exchange of ideas. We have already talked of the necessity of detachment, of seeing the patient as a creature in God's care, for whom God alone is ultimately responsible. From this stillness of spirit can come a word picked clean of pretence, not words which spring from compulsion, but a word which comes from admitting the personal mystery of another in suffering and from becoming aware of the compassion of God welling up in the midst of one's own inability to do anything good without him. Every time we speak from silence we convey that our words are no less than a compassionate grasping after mystery: 'For silence is not God, nor speaking. . . He is hidden between them, and cannot be found by anything your soul does, but only by the love of your heart'.[17]

How we speak says just as much as what we say. It is not that we can speak truth when love is absent; the only way the truth can be spoken is in love. There can be no formula for this, and it would be misleading to isolate any aspect of truth's language – rest, tone, rhythm, pitch – because that would be to trap God's freedom in musical technique. It is better to talk of a costly discipline to be learned. W.H. Vanstone makes comparison with the activity of a lover or an artist, whose 'aspiration is not to express *himself* but to express responsive love. Therefore he may not use whatever form or symbol comes most naturally to himself and is least demanding upon himself'.[18] Everything will come right when the pastor truly loves her friend, when she learns to lay down her life in word and deed, a condition brilliantly captured by Elizabeth Jennings in her poem 'Let Things Alone':

> You have to learn it all over again,
> The words, the sounds, almost the whole language
> Because this is a time when words must be strict and new
> Not concerning you,
> Or only indirectly,
> Concerning a pain
> Learnt as most people sometime or other learn it
> With shock, then dark.[19]

Speaking out of listening will usually mean that the starting point of conversation will be the patient's feelings about his illness. The patient is used to rehearsing his condition before medical staff. The pastor signals her intent to be other than a carer, however, by listening on, beyond the immediate circumstances, to stories from the past, opinions, dreams, even to the latest gossip, in a total concern for the whole person. In this conversation the patient may not, at first, expect enlightenment about anything in particular. If he finds the listener trustworthy, however, the story will be retold in an altogether more searching, tentative way; the pastor is being invited to gather together at least some of the strands of that person's unique bodily story in a loving judgement. Wherever filial openness to God grows, there the Holy Spirit can come bringing what St John sees as the only divine gift, 'grace of the truth', which is 'the revelation of the Fatherhood of God by the Sonship of Jesus, and of the possibility for men themselves to go to the Father, to become children of God.'[20]

This means that any word of truth that is spoken in the encounter by the pastor will be one that not only speaks of the love of the Father but also one which, in some way or other, makes sense of the patient's biography, helping the search for meaning and affirming bodily existence. This affirmation of a person's bodily story is possible only within an *unconditional* affirmation of the unique value of the dying person. The pastor certainly does not have a monopoly on the sort of friendship which is the source of the word of truth. At best, she finds her place among all others whose concern is the patient's bodily welfare and who cherish the body.[21] Her speaking the truth (part of the truth that will be spoken by all who love) can only happen because a team has brought bodily pain under control. The team provides a credible ground for the Christian gospel of the resurrection of the body, for they who cherish the body point beyond to God's utter commitment to the material world revealed in the Word's becoming flesh.

I heard of one instance where it took one and a half hours for the nursing staff to clean and dress someone's cancerous and septic toe. I also saw a nurse who calmed a delirious man through her soothing words of concern and her stroking of his hair. Even after death the body is respected. When I was taken to see a dead body and said that it seemed like a shell, a nurse attending it angrily replied, 'But we treat it like a person!'

Confrontation and the Arrival of Hope

Once again speaking and touch have become intertwined. But while the pastor comforts the whole patient in a bodily way, she cannot speak the truth by mumbling a woolly yes towards another's story. The Greek Fathers of the Church insisted that 'truth should be fully applied to existence, thereby making life something true, i.e. undying'.[22] Only personal challenge, delivered in the context of a secure relationship, can help a patient beyond his assumptions.[23] For Jesus, his speaking of the truth continually led him into confrontation. His own people were not willing to receive the truth he brought (1:11). Their defences were so strong that even his curing of a blind man could not dispel a charge of demon-possession (10:21). His disciples, also, had to be confronted, as we have seen after Peter's refusal of Jesus' washing, because unless they did accept the truth about themselves they could have no share in his life (13:8). Because Peter had not realised his complete inability to save himself, he was bound to suffer until Christ's word cleansed him. Those who now suffer in the face of death also need to hear the truth. Henri Nouwen has important words about challenge: 'ministry is a very confronting service. It does not allow others to live with illusions of immortality and wholeness. It keeps reminding others that they are mortal and broken, but also that with the recognition of this condition, liberation starts'.[24]

Don: Why am I so tired?
RR: Because you're ill.
Don: Oh!

The last days of life will rarely be the place where confrontation with the self-righteous will be fruitful, but there are those who will benefit from the truth being set against their ignorance or fear in a loving way, without aggression. This is what confrontation is. It is a necessary aspect of serving by speaking the truth in love. Love should never be mistaken for indulgence, nor responsiveness for passivity. Confrontation will happen wherever integrity engages with illusion. Alistair Campbell reminds us that 'the person of integrity is first and foremost a critic of self, of tendencies to self-deception and escape from reality, of desire for false inner security in place of the confrontation with truth which integrity demands.'[25] A person like this will be unable to reinforce another's defences against the truth; her being and relating will challenge unreality whenever it is met.

Confrontation fits in with the wider process of responding to another's story. As we have said, a patient will often share, in greater or lesser detail, the story of his life, as part of the search for meaning. As the story is presented, the pastor listens actively, offering comment on it as seems right. Sometimes she may confront with a humorous remark,[26] sometimes she may share part of her own story. The resulting challenge is often indirect, inviting people to step from behind their defences into freedom rather than cause them to retreat still further (4:10,16). Those who speak what they have heard from the Father will offer an original[27] word, which will become a vehicle by which Truth breaks into the story, offering new self-understanding.

Defences are a barrier to truth. Though they cannot ever be encouraged by anyone seeking to witness to Jesus Christ, they must be understood and respected. Defences are ways of coping independently with loss of personal hope, though they may be supported from outside by a conspiracy of the wider community. Even in a hospice, whose purposes are known, defences can remain strong; relief from pain can be taken for recovery or eternal remission (and even the presence of a pastor may signal the possibility of a magical cure). The pastor, while respecting human frailty as a true friend would, cannot join the plot against reality, whatever the personal cost. Alistair Campbell puts it well:

> When someone is desperately asking us to help them deny the reality of their pain, it requires great strength to stay silent. Yet silence is often our greatest service. By

remaining *with* people, but at the same time refusing to take the escape from pain they seek, we can restore their courage to voice their deepest fears and express the anguish they find so threatening.[28]

In refusing to conspire the pastor is offering a new way forward, and by her unflinching presence she also invites the patient to step out from behind his defences onto the path of truth, which though unfamiliar need never be trodden alone.

There are no rules as to what should be said when it is right to speak. Rumbold points out that the giving of mere information is not enough.[29] Confrontation does not mean throwing medical facts into the face of the terminally ill; it is a call to turn from illusion made through the presence of those who already have hope. Denial is a turning away from God to seek immortality in self-deception; the way to hope is to find eternal life in shared truth. The psychiatrist Avery Weisman has grouped the defences of the dying into three categories, which Rumbold has discussed in relation to the emergence of hope:[30]

First order: denying the primary facts of the illness the symptoms.
*   admission → hope *for* recovery
Second order: denying the inferences to be drawn from the symptoms.
**   admission → hope *that* . . . simple, personal hopes
Third order: denying the possibility of extinction, of death being the end of existence.
*** admission → hope *in* . . . mature, transcendent hope

Hope can only emerge as the various orders of denial break down and truth is admitted at different levels (marked by asterisks). If a patient is given the freedom to admit the facts of the illness then hope *for* recovery may develop. In hospitals, the path often stops here, with second order denial linked to first order hope: our society says it is almost always better to hope for life than to face death; but only if second order denial is broken down can second order hope emerge, whose nature is hope *that*. These are simple, personal hopes that, for example, the patient will be able to die with dignity or that he will be remembered fondly by his children. A pastor must be careful here not to bolster hope of immortality with religious concepts, because only once a patient has realised the finality of death can mature hope develop, that is, hope *in*, an attitude of trust, which says yes to all that has been and sees in the past and present a Beyond.

We can see that both crisis and community are integral parts of the journey into hope; without them, patients would rest in illusion. Weisman's theoretical analysis does not, however, suggest what should be said. How much more difficult it is to know what to say in practice, where meaning is sought more in sign and symbol than in statement. We can say, at least, that the pastor must be there, sharing the story, not saying the superficial but pointing to the truth in word and deed, even when a patient shrinks back through fear. Always, a pastor's presence should be sign that it is all right to explore any avenue, silently or in conversation; but that the patient need never journey alone. The cost of this is enormous, as Dr Sheila Cassidy testifies:

> Joy and I engaged in dialogue. I do not recall exactly how it went, except that I spoke gently and truthfully, responding as sensitively as I was able to her questions, overt and hidden. When I had finished, there was a bond between us that was never broken − an indefinable link between two people facing the unknown. I was completely spent. Such conversations are extremely demanding in terms of intuition and sensitivity, for one is tailoring one's conversation to the language and needs of the individual, moving as in a dance − now leading, now following, but always listening to the music.[31]

This quotation begs to be juxtaposed with another from Mother Mary Clare who says:

> The one who is being sent, the apostle, . . . is sent to give himself, just as the Son was sent by the Father to give

himself for the life of the world. The apostle is one who is sent to be spent. Thus, when we talk about apostles . . . we are not talking about a pipeline, or a relay race, but about a universal dance in which mankind is being taken up . . . into the sacrificial love which is the life of the triune God.[32]

The two quotations taken together emphasise the immense cost of joining in the dance. The step cannot be followed either by holding back or by lunging forward. The whole self, body and mind, must be given to the music. That is why preparation of the highest order is needed, such as is suggested by Mother Mary Clare's words. Only those who in stillness have been gathered into Christ's givenness to the Father, only those who have known his filial response piercing the darkness of their hearts can know how to take the hand of another who fears and share the path by which they together will be led into truth. Often the dance culminates very literally in this way: the patient accepts the pastor's hand and her offer of prayer; the pastor gathers the patient's life into words, which are given by the Spirit as she prays; these words become a vehicle by which the patient can redirect the mixed voices of his heart outwards, confronting self-deceit, entrusting his story to the Truth whom both are seeking. Praying together, therefore, can be the supreme act of communion, and of revelation.

A moving story told by a hospital chaplain, the Revd Dr Anne Townsend, hardly needs comment; but I shall discuss some of its themes as a way of concluding this survey of how a pastor can forge communion and the revelation of truth within community.

More than One Name for Eternity

I had spent hours earlier this year sitting by Jean's bed, stroking her arm, and listening to her sharing her painful feelings about the cancer which was eating its way through her body. At first there seemed little to talk about. Her life in her inner-city high-rise flat, her work

selling fish from a market stall, and her desertion by several men differed vastly from my commuterland existence.

Of church and God we never spoke, for this was frightening, alien territory to her. And yet, week after week, she asked for me – a hospital chaplain – to sit with her. After several weeks of this (we talked about her cat), I was really clear in my own mind that she really did want me there as a *chaplain* – and that the God of whom we rarely spoke directly was very close in our encounters (unless my words, 'God bless!' counted for more than I knew).

At last to my joy and relief, we discovered shared territory: Southend-on-Sea. It was the place to which she had gone as a child for joyful family outings, it was the place where her husband had courted her for months, it was the place where for the first time she had marvelled at the sea's clear vastness after her cramped inner-city environment. I had started married life in Southend; our first child had been born there. Southend for Jean was a place of escape from life's harsh realities; it spelled joy, peace and fun. It was, for me, a place of endings of old ways of living and the beginning of new ones.

As Jean grew progressively weaker, and her pain harder to bear, we would go together in imagination to Southend. We'd walk along the pier, buy cockles and winkles and candyfloss, and join the crowds watching Punch and Judy or listening to the band. 'Going to Southend' became an activity important to both of us. Mysteriously it somehow seemed to begin to hold out hope to her that the end of her despair, pain and hopelessness just might be something that could only be described as 'good'. Hope like this was crucial both to her and also to me, as I sat feeling helpless close to her hopelessness.

On the morning I was due to leave for holiday, I went to say goodbye to Jean. She looked more defeated and destroyed by her cancer than ever, her eyes were

wounded and no longer able to weep, her hand cold and
moist. She clung on to me tightly: 'We keep on talking
about Southend', she said. 'Am I ever going to get there
in the end . . . or will I get lost on the way?' I took a
deep breath, swallowing back the tears that threatened
to overwhelm me. 'You'll be there very soon, Jean . . .
that *other* Southend is quite close now . . . not too far to
go.' Her face relaxed, she closed her eyes and I knew
that she had understood what I had not spelled out for
her. I kissed her goodbye. On return from holiday I
heard that she had died just two hours after I had left
her.

Jean and I learned to love one another, and our differences made this a kind of miracle. But the legacy she left
me is even more precious: she taught me that eternity
can be spoken of in a language I would never have
thought of using.[33]

First we notice the place of time in the encounter. Caring
for Jean was not a full-time occupation for Anne Townsend.
She visited when she was called for and, one assumes, at other
times. When they were together the time was spent in being
together, sharing the length of time available in an unhurried
way. These times added up to hours of caring over several
weeks. A gentle and non-threatening touch encouraged a
friendship in which words were not easily found, at least at
first. Jean struggled to express her pain and fear while Anne
tried to listen and understand a vastly different life. Anne did
not make the mistake of identifying her feelings of helplessness
with Jean's of hopelessness. (The difference in their feeling is
also seen when Jean's vulnerability is met by Anne's tears.)
Her struggle was not to judge the life unfolding before her
but to love and to find the common ground on which love
could be communicated through words. The language that
was eventually found sprung from a listening and loving
bodily friendship.

In this striving for communion God was present. Anne, as
chaplain, stood as the only link Jean had with an unfamiliar

and frightening concept. Her listening allowed Jean the freedom to open out her story to another. Jean could not manage
a God apart from the life she had lived, but events proved
that she was searching for something beyond life and above
the peace, joy and fun she had known. Anne's presence as a
friend gave a frightening concept a human face; more than
that, this human face valued her bodily life. The God behind
Anne was interested in coming into Jean's familiar and
beloved territory.

Within the ground of friendship trust grew, and with trust
came the ability to share fantasy and desire. It is no accident,
then, that a language of hope grew up between Anne and
Jean in the communion of the Holy Spirit. The Holy Spirit
created an inner language between them, behind ordinary
words, as their common search for common ground bore fruit,
at the place where their bodily stories converged and at a
depth which could support suffering and keep hope alive.
The language was usable by God because it had been used
concretely to refer to a shared human story and had been an
expression of love. This dance of love-in-language reached its
climax in Jean's outburst of fear and yearning trust, and in
Anne's reply. The familiar code held no fear and provoked
no misleading concepts; instead it could convey all the grace
of God: 'no you won't get lost' – God loves you and has a
home for you in the peace and joy and fun you so desire. In
a moment of simplicity for which it cost so much to prepare,
the truth was spoken and received in human meeting: the
Word was made flesh.

4

SUFFERING AND SALVATION –
THE GIFT OFFERED

The central purpose of the hospice movement is to offer victory over suffering and death to its patients. Both Chapters 4 and 5 are devoted to considering what victory might mean to the terminally ill and how it can be won. Though we have argued that patients and their family should be allowed the freedom to deny death's coming,[1] we have also seen that hospice care offers a tide of acceptance and hope which draws them in the opposite direction towards truth. Hospice care is intended to help those who are treading an often lonely path towards death to end their days with dignity and with an answer to the threat they face.

We start this chapter by trying to understand the suffering that terminally ill people may endure. It arises from a combination of bodily, mental and emotional needs. To overcome this depth of suffering would be victory indeed; the question is whether John's Gospel has anything to offer those who are looking for victory over death, or is the Jesus portrayed there unrelated to frail, human life? We shall discover that there is every connection to be made between the life of Christ and those who follow him, especially in a meditation on the saying of the Good Shepherd who lays down his life for the sheep. Christ's death is a supreme act of self-giving to the Father. So his death is not a defeat but a fulfilment of a life lived outwards in 'ecstasy'.

Though ecstasy, like victory, is an extreme word and indeed one open to misinterpretation, it expresses well the joy and triumph of someone whose whole being discovers freedom in the midst of suffering. Dying presents the supreme threat to the self that exists by itself and for itself. Yet, in answering the call of Love to follow Christ into darkness, this unfinished self can, as it were, burst its boundaries to stand complete in the perfect sacrifice of Christ. In responding to the One who leads his sheep into the pasture of communion with the Father, the broken are made whole.

As an example of how the risen Christ offers eternal communion to his disciples we listen to the story of the calling of Peter in John 21. This sets the stage for the next chapter which looks at what a patient needs to do to receive victory. We start, though, by bringing together the suffering of the dying with the Passion of Christ.

Human Suffering and the Question of Meaning

Terminally ill patients have many bodily, mental and emotional needs, which vary from patient to patient but which in every case are interrelated. Extreme pain, to someone suffering it, is totally engrossing. Drugs can be found; but even when pain is 'managed' the body exists in unstable equilibrium, making the sufferer aware of the possibility of attack (though self-administration of drugs can help this). The patient must face a body which is no longer the same outside self, frailer, increasingly dependent on others and sometimes disfigured. So the mind must cope with the threat of pain and the indignity of the diminution of the body, even as it may be becoming increasingly slow or confused. The patient may become anxious, angry or depressed as control slips from mind and body. In the last stages of illness there may be a general shrinking of consciousness, concentration and co-ordination, contributing to an increase in vulnerability, a lowered self-esteem and, most importantly, to a loss of identity.

Beyond the fact of losing control, patients are confronted with questions of meaning and value. Now a patient must be taking leave of her work, her friends and family, what is the significance of the memories and achievements of the past and of the present, precious experience of being alive? Is there any purpose to what has gone before and to what is coming? The totality of this suffering – the fact of it and the demand it makes for interpretation – may be termed 'spiritual' suffering. Using the picture of human being we outlined in Chapter 1 we can say that the spiritual suffering brought about by the imminence of death is the condition of the human heart which can find no answer to the needs of mind and body.

There are many different models of the process of how patients may overcome the threat of death. Common to all of them, however, is the idea about what *finally* needs to happen for the patient to die well: 'we achieve peace by facing and accepting the reality of our own death'.[2] This means that, however important is denial or bargaining as a defence mechanism, a dying person can only be set free by a truth which addresses her own mortality. This process has to go to the depths of human being because truth has to enable a person to transcend the need to exist, for physical death is real and final.

I was taken into the room where the bodies of those who had died were prepared to be viewed by their family and friends. I did not really know what to expect. I had shared a joke with Lilian the day before, but now I saw and felt what seemed to be a yellowing, pliant doll; hair neatly brushed back, a cold hand placed over the sheets for the purpose of touching – so much smaller and utterly lacking in life.

No one will step into the darkness willingly and knowingly unless she has won the battle to find meaning in the face of death. The metaphor of 'victory' is not, therefore, an over-dramatic one, though whether victory is anything more than a metaphor must be judged by studying John's Gospel.

Victory over Suffering in John's Gospel

John's Gospel, at first, hardly seems a good place to look for help for those who suffer. An influential theologian, Ernst Käsemann, argued that the Johannine Jesus is hardly human:

> In what sense is the flesh, who walks on water and through closed door, who cannot be captured by his

enemies, who at the well of Samaria is tired and desires
a drink, yet has no need of drink and has food different
from that which his disciples seek? He permits Lazarus
to lie in the grave for four days in order that the miracle
of his resurrection may be more impressive. . . And in
the end the Johannine Christ goes victoriously to his
death of his own accord.[3]

Käsemann's rhetoric, however, springs from a limited view
of what it might mean to be human and glorified. Jesus'
approach to the death of his friend Lazarus has already been
interpreted in human terms in Chapter 2's study of detachment. Now we shall look at Jesus' approach to his own death
to see where patients can find victory as they face their own
passion.

We are quite entitled to an answer to spiritual suffering in
John's Gospel, for it starts with the thundering assertion, 'In
him was life', which J.V. Taylor calls 'the most theologically
mature pronouncement about Christ in the New Testament'.[4]
The evangelist sets out his stall from the beginning: there is
a way by which the problem of human mortality can be
addressed; and the Gospel goes on to make its appeal directly
to those who face a comprehensive threat, external and
internal. In the face of the world's hatred and persecution
and of their own human frailty, readers are given answers to
the threat of being scattered and of losing faith (14:1, 16:33).
There is no mistaking the fact, either, that Jesus does not
remain aloof; he suffers – in his own way. Once again this is
signalled right at the outset of the Gospel, where the irony of
his mission is summed up, 'He came to his own and his own
people did not accept him' (1:11). Jesus knows so much the
truth of his own words, but not only the Jews in general but
also those Jews who supported him failed to understand him.
His tears at Bethany testify to that (11:35). The undercurrent
of struggle comes most to the surface at 12:27:

> Now my soul is troubled.
> What shall I say:
> Father, save me from this hour?

> But it is for this very reason that I have come
>   to this hour.
> Father, glorify your name!

This is more than a mental conflict over his own fate; it is
Christ coming to terms with the scope of his mission, which
is to face the hour of his death. The point is not that Jesus
can dodge suffering but precisely that he must suffer and that
he knows that he must suffer, and in saying yes to the cup
his Father offers he fulfils the whole purpose of his coming
and overcomes the world. He is not alone, because the Father
is with him (12:28b, 16:32). So Jesus can meet his hour with
serenity. At the confrontation in the Garden, Jesus, far from
retreating as the crowd comes to arrest him, steps forward to
proclaim, 'I am he', majestic words from the One who is not
afraid to be the Sufferer (18:4,6). On the journey to Calvary,
Jesus carries the cross for himself (19:17), choosing a cross
which he had no choice but to take, as 'the privileged instru-
ment of his work of salvation, the sign of his triumph and his
sovereignty'.[5]

De la Potterie, an eminent Jesuit biblical scholar, details
how the account of the Passion in John's Gospel differs from
the other, 'synoptic' Gospels. There is no agony in Gethsem-
ane, no kiss from Judas, no flight of the disciples, no trial
before the Sanhedrin, no mockeries, injuries, spittings, no
hitting on the head with the reed, no cry of despair from
the cross and no mention of darkness when Christ dies.[6] All
attention is focused on the Man who has triumphed over his
suffering by staying obedient to the Father. Suffering, however, is still the background of the Passion story from which
the victorious Messiah rises in relief. John's persistent irony
continues to point up a victory which looked mock-worthy to
the outsider. In this ironic vein, it is Pilate, who has dismissed
the notion of truth, who speaks truly in dialogue with the
crowd: ' "Here is your king," said Pilate to the Jews. But they
shouted, "Away with him, away with him, crucify him."
Pilate said, "Shall I crucify your king?" The chief priests
answered, "We have no king except Caesar" ' (19:14b,15).

Right up to his last breath Jesus suffers, thirsting for the Spirit to be poured out on human flesh, from his broken body. His victory cry, 'It is fulfilled!', is the last word of a man who knows he has done his Father's will to the end, by his obedience through suffering. The victory is real because so was the battle (16:21).

But how does the Messiah find victory within his suffering while remaining in undeserved pain, and how, if at all, is this related to the needs of the terminally ill now? Both these questions can be addressed by a detailed study of John 10, where we are given insight into the heart of the good shepherd and also into his relationship to the sheep.

Suffering and the Call of Love

The good shepherd, Christ says, speaking of himself, comes to save his sheep from threat. He comes with true authority 'from above', and, having no need of deceit, can approach the sheepfold openly. (The doorkeeper recognises this authority and lets the shepherd in.) Once among the sheep his authority is exercised in the care by which he gathers his own. Jesus is the *good* shepherd, whom his sheep follow willingly. Others have broken into the fold – leaders of state and religion – who have been concerned only for themselves. These false shepherds are thieves and robbers who have brought nothing but destruction to the sheep. The good shepherd, however, comes to restore the flock. He helps them in their need, stepping right among the sheep to bring them out from where they wait. He calls his sheep by name – each is summoned personally to follow him. His sheep recognise his voice as the voice of a friend, not a stranger, and they follow him out of trust. Without this shepherd there would be nowhere for the sheep to go, only for them the prospect of further oppression. And so more than being the shepherd, Christ is even the door of the sheepfold, the way by which his flock find safe passage to pasture.

Already the simple, pastoral image of a shepherd calling his flock out from among many in a fold cannot enclose the meaning of Jesus' words. He is both shepherd and door for the sheep. He offers to them, one by one, an exclusive and all-embracing deliverance, far greater than a shepherd's care and protection. The shepherd, unlike a hireling, can be counted on not to abandon the sheep when he sees the wolf coming. He may even be killed in the course of defending the sheep from danger; but only Christ, the good shepherd, willingly and knowingly gives his life for the sheep. His sheep do not ask that he should lay down his life, neither does the danger of their being scattered determine it. He lays down his life because in the command received from the Father he finds his freedom. He lays down his life because the sheep, by the Father's gift, are his to save.

Jesus' conscious offering of his life for the sheep is a supreme act of majesty: 'No one takes it from me; I lay it down of my own free will.' It shows him to be not only shepherd but king, a shepherd-king in the line of the great King David. In the life of Jesus, authority and obedience, victory and self-sacrifice are one. This life, received from the Father, is always his by right in his Father's love. The mission of the good shepherd is to give this very life to the sheep. They receive it through their obeying his kingly call and submitting to his kingly authority – through faith in him – and yet he always remains a shepherd, whose voice is the voice of a friend and whose offering of life leads them into pasture.

The deliverance brought by the shepherd-king breaks the bounds between time and eternity. Only gradually, though, does the true nature of his mission become apparent. The scene at first is of a shepherd who comes with authority to the sheepfold, and of the sheep who hear his voice. Within that scene the shepherd makes a personal relationship with his own sheep. He calls them by name and they recognise his voice. He leads them out and they follow because they know his voice. The shepherd-sheep relationship is not yet fully drawn. Then, new dimensions of dependence, freedom and security are opened up. Jesus is the door. The sheep depend entirely on him for their deliverance; but any who come into the fold through him will find a freedom beyond following:

gathered into one flock each will be safe and free to find pasture.

While the picture of Christ as the door sheds new light on Christ's relationship with the sheep, it also, for a moment, makes it appear less than personal. The eternal depth of Jesus' relationship with his followers is hidden, until he goes on to explain the meaning of the laying down of his life. Christ goes ahead of his flock, leading them through death and resurrection to eternal life. The good shepherd lays down his life for the sheep, not staying on earth to protect them from physical harm, but going ahead, to bring safe pasture to those who know him. In the world they will have suffering; but they will also have his victory, because as sheep of the shepherd they have an inner relationship with him on which they can feed. Whether in or out of immediate danger, they rest secure, because they may graze on the life which has gone triumphantly through death, the life of the shepherd-king who has overcome the world and who now dwells among his sheep, and within them.

The shepherd's going ahead and laying down of life, the sheep's following – these images point to a relationship which Christ initiates. But once established, the communion on which his followers feed admits no junior partners: 'I know my own and my own know me, just as the Father knows me and I know the Father,' Jesus says. Here the saving relationship between Christ and his followers is revealed in all its fullness. Here is eternal life shared between shepherd and sheep, as it is and always has been shared between Father and Son. In this bond of mutual knowing there is no inequality between one and the other. Christ lays down his life not as a shepherd among sheep but as a Friend among friends. He is as much one with them as he is with the Father; and so he dies for them, knowing their need as his own and seeing in their need the will of the Father. He loves the sheep with the same total love as he gives to the Father. His self-sacrifice, then, is a shepherdly and majestic act of love, made for those he knows in the freedom of obeying the One who knows him. The life he lays down and receives back for his own is pasture indeed, a life of unbroken communion with the Father; not a security zone, but a divine embrace from which no person or power can snatch them. In this communion, Christ's friends find eternal fulfilment in their being known and knowing, being loved and loving. In the one flock, they share in Christ what Christ shares eternally with the Father.

The Human Search and Divine Salvation

Self-abandonment is the key to understanding the victory of Jesus over suffering and death in John's Gospel. His death on the cross is no more or less than the culmination of a life lived outside the bounds of itself, a life lived in 'ecstasy', where Christ is joined to the Father in a holy union of knowledge and obedience. From the beginning of the Gospel, Christ is shown to be living within the knowledge of the Father's love and also of his coming hour. In knowing what he does, he is able to abandon himself to the life he is given to live and to share with his own. Jesus is a fully awakened Messiah who is called by the Father to speak his words (14:10). He is the Son, who embodies all his Father is or does (14:9). God is the source of his being (8:42). The parable of the shepherd of the sheep illuminates the vocation of Jesus hinted at in the very first exchange with the disciples – 'Rabbi, where do you live?' 'Come and see' (1:38). His home is with the Father and he comes to lead others into this true pasture. Jesus' talk of his being a willing victim for the sheep is placed in the Gospel directly before the events of history move inexorably forward to his hour. The passion is no accident (13:3). Christ is in command of his oblation. He himself decides when he should speak (19:10), even when he should die (19:28). The good shepherd is not having his life taken from him: he is willingly giving it away, out of love.

Christ's knowledge cannot be divorced from his obedience. Only in obeying his Father's call to death does Christ maintain the divine communion which existed before all creation (4:34; 16:33). Through his obedience, Christ carries in his body this divine-love to his friends. 'The profound reason for the Incarnation does not come from man but from God, from his desire to become Man and to make of humanity a theophany, the beloved ground of His presence'.[7] In the person of Jesus himself we see that divine love can fully meet the human search for salvation. But more than that, John shows us that in Jesus human love can satisfy God's desire to save his people: 'the cross is not a reaction wrung from God by man's sin but God being himself, totally abandoned for the life of his children'.[8] In the meditation on the Good Shepherd we used biblical terms. Jesus' death is an act of majesty, a shepherdly act of care or gathering, and the act of an obedient servant.

All these terms are part of one reality, one human and divine movement of ecstasy, a union of offering in which the Father and the Son are joined in an ineffable bond of joy and overflowing love. We see its mystery in the necessity of the cross, here expressed in a stanza from one of the medieval Passion plays. At the foot of the cross, the beloved disciple comforts the Mother of Jesus:

> Gentle Lady,
> It was his will that he should suffer savage pain,
> And die upon a tree
> And to life would rise again
> And on the third day it would be.
> Love made thy Son endure for us:
> Remember he said all would be thus;
> All this he vowed before.
> Alas, to me and many more
> He was a good master.

We are now ready to connect this interpretation of Jesus' death as a saving act of divine love with the search of the dying for meaning. Dying is a most complex process which rarely progresses in a predictable pattern. In Chapter 1, however, I have already made some comment on a general search of the dying for identity. A person facing the loss of her body faces the end of her biography, the story of her bodily self. She also faces the end of receiving the love offered by others to her bodily self. We may now put these ideas together by saying that a person's biography, which holds her sense of self, is essentially a search for love. Philip Larkin puts it this way:

> . . . in everyone there sleeps
> A sense of life lived according to love.
> To some it means the difference they could make
> By loving others, but across most it sweeps
> As all they might have done had they been loved.
> That nothing cures.[9]

It is interesting that a male poet should have written this, for there is some evidence that men in Western society tend to consider their life in terms of its meaning while women measure it more by the relationships formed within it.[10] In the end these are two different ways of approaching the same principle of love, one working from the word to the flesh and the other from the flesh to the word. Both are contained in the approach taken here, for a search for love begs the question of meaning and also assumes an experience of love fulfilled in varying degrees.

Larkin's poem points to what Christian theology holds as a universal truth: women and men have been made in the image of Love, for God is love, and every human being needs to be saved from lovelessness. The self is an unfinished mask, a persona, looking to be completed beyond itself by another: 'no human I can awaken to itself unless it is addressed as You by another I'.[11] Those facing death have the opportunity to realise that their life can only make sense if death is in some sense our human vocation, a way by which the strands of existence can be drawn together into an eternal fullness. The connection has to be made, therefore, between death and love, not through an act of the mind but of the whole being. The theologian Hans von Balthasar supplies the key: 'Death can, as it were, bring together the whole of existence in which *self-abandonment* and an intimation of the sense of love hidden in being itself occurs'.[12]

This, as we have seen in the meditation on John 10, happened supremely in the life of Jesus. His cry, 'It is finished!' from his throne of agony is a sign of the ecstasy of the Sufferer defeating death. His whole attention and being is directed outwards to the need of his friends (19:26,27) and to the will of his Father (19:28). His words are not the easy, triumphant cry of a demigod, styled by the evangelist for literary and theological reasons. The mission of Christ is completed in the 'giving up of the spirit' for the sheep. John coins this special phrase to highlight the unity and fruitfulness of the one, divine and human offering of the whole person of Christ. In ecstasy, Jesus willingly and knowingly gives his whole life back to the Father. He bows his head in submission to the Father and finds rest for humanity. He gives up the spirit so that the Spirit is given. Death is transcended in, and by, the totally human life of a faithful son, whose awareness and complete obedience culminate in a love that reaches beyond death by crucifixion to the call of the Father. In the one person of Jesus Christ, humanity and divinity are uniquely united in a complete love, a complete response, which is stronger even than death.

John's good news is that this human ecstasy of complete self-giving is available through the Spirit to all who believe in God's Word. The next chapter will focus on the response to the Word that is necessary to bring a victory of rest to terminally ill people, which we shall call the work of 'letting go'. At the end of this survey of the ecstasy between the Son and the Father, however, we must be clear that Christ's perfect response to Love's call is the God-given foundation of all subsequent, imperfect ones. To this end, we look at one of the resurrection stories.

The resurrection of Christ was the Father's faithful response to the faithful offering of his beloved son. The Father's personal vindication of the Son did not stop at the raising of Jesus from the dead, for the Son did not die on his own behalf. In the resurrection, the Father gave Jesus back to his friends so that Jesus' love could be fulfilled by finding its response among those given to him by the Father. So this chapter concludes by connecting the parable of John 10 with the story in the final chapter of the Gospel, where Jesus calls Peter to follow him.

The Shepherd Gives Life

Christ risen from the dead comes to call his own by name. After breakfast by the Sea of Tiberias, he singles out Peter from among the disciples. Much ink has been spilled over whether this passage supports the tradition of Peter's primacy in the Church, but Jesus' choice of Peter represents first and foremost a personal call to follow. For the good of the flock he has to be shown the way forward. Peter is still leading the group but he is aimless. He is living with a restless heart, wandering back to his old existence as a fisherman. The one who has denied Jesus three times needs to rediscover the truth for which he can live and die. So Jesus returns to Peter beyond death to call him to himself. He does not come to show up his friend's failure. His voice is the voice of a friend, which gives Peter the freedom to follow out of trust.

The conversation between Jesus and Peter is a real one. The friend who stands before him knows him better than he knows himself – so Jesus' prediction of his denial proved. Peter must now search his heart and say whether he does love the one who stands before him. The threefold pattern of Jesus' questioning invites Simon son of John to make a new start by transcending his past. As Peter owns his love for Christ in all its fragility he receives from him a command, 'Feed my lambs.' It is not thrust upon him, but laid before him as the way by which he himself will realise his love for the Lord. Jesus, knowing that Peter will follow this time, solemnly promises that in feeding his sheep Peter will suffer loss of bodily control and be put to death. For Peter, though, the call of the risen Lord is the door onto his own true life. The promise of martyrdom is desirable because in Christ's presence it is seen to be the promise of eternal pasture. He, too, can follow the way of the good shepherd into resurrection life. The way is set for Peter to feed Jesus' sheep by willingly offering his life for them.

John's Gospel does not give us the end to Peter's story. What is given is an outline of how spiritual suffering is overcome. The human heart must grow in the presence of the risen

Christ. The shepherd's authority is seen in the power of his word to extrude the deepest desire of his sheep, to love and be loved, to know and be known. His friendship can bring self-knowledge and joy to those in danger of slipping back into mere existence and enable them to find meaning by which to face suffering and death.

The collect for the fourth Sunday after Easter points to the gap which must be crossed if victory is to be won in any human life, the crossing of which we are now set to explore.

> Almighty God,
> who alone can bring order
> to the unruly wills and passions of sinful men:
> give us grace
> to love what you command
> and to desire what you promise,
> that in all the changes and chances of this world,
> our hearts may surely there be fixed
> where lasting joys are to be found;
> through Jesus Christ our Lord.

5

VICTORY THROUGH DEATH –
THE GIFT RECEIVED

By choosing the word 'ecstasy' in the last chapter to describe Christ's self-abandonment on the cross we began to forge a human connection between Christ's Passion and the suffering of the terminally ill. His suffering and death were the culmination of an ec-static life, that is, of a life lived in communion with the Father *standing outside* the bounds of egoism. He was ever one with the Father, never an isolated individual out of sorts with the fount of his being. So now the argument continues: the Good Shepherd's ecstasy has, through the Spirit, opened the way for all his sheep to find eternal pasture, the end of all human desire and the fulfilment of all personal hope. Once coming to know a true ecstasy of love, a human being transcends the need to exist and is able to die with serenity.

This chapter attempts to put down a few markers along the path of ecstasy, all the time bearing in mind the uniqueness of each person's dying. A look at John 12:23ff provides a definition for the 'letting go' talked about in the literature on dying. It is an ecstatic movement starting from the will in which one's whole life – body, mind and spirit – is offered to God. This means death for the ego, that is, an end to the self which seeks existence outside the knowledge and love of God. Letting go is not easy. It involves a struggle to trust in God. Changes must happen at a spiritual rather than a merely psychological level: the heart must grow and the spirit be raised in the Spirit.

Beyond struggle, patients can find a new identity as those

whose deepest self is a gift of Love. Sons and daughters of God are free to die well, because they know the truth. Human restlessness is, in essence, an expression of the desire to transcend the bounds of finitude and egoism and to find communion. Some call this desire 'eros' and hold it in suspicion,[1] partly because they define it too narrowly as a love-of-things or as an exclusively sexual love, partly because of its destructive manifestations in the taking of narcotics,[2] in promiscuity or acquisitiveness, for example. But eros is a friend of faith, and the perversion of eros points all the more to its power in human life and the urgency of the need to slake the thirst for oneness within the perfect ecstasy of God. As Augustine of Hippo said, 'You made us for yourself, and our heart is restless until it finds its rest in you.'[3]

Beyond the darkness of suffering there lies a new story whose central character is God. Mary of Magdala's story in John 20 illustrates the connection between the new life and the old. In encounter with the risen Christ her past, even her religious past, is transcended. Her example shows how eros, once transformed, can find a home in God and also that struggle is a usually necessary but not a sufficient condition for the truth to be received from above. When patients can say yes to the One who calls beyond the darkness, they will know eternal life and an end to their spiritual suffering, because they will have the hope of children of God in the eternal love of their Father.

Letting Go, the Way into Life

Death is a complete separation.[4] Dying is the process of being stripped of all that one can give up in this world. The question is whether life will be prized from a clenched and shaking fist or whether it will be offered open-handedly in love. A good death cannot be defined primarily by outward signs. The cliché of 'dying peacefully' can just as easily describe a death under strong sedation or a patient's sad resignation to fate as it can a final coming to terms with life. Conversely, a dying which does not proceed smoothly in an institutional sense may well be a sign of an engagement with a new, disturbing reality, a real 'letting go'. Ainsworth-Smith and Speck begin to capture the force of this 'double-edged expression. It can imply being drawn gently into a new sort of existence; or being released or dragged into a void where nothing is safe or consistent'.[5] This chapter will therefore probe the inner activity of the heart, rather than try to pin down significant words and actions. This makes sense if, as was the conclusion of the last chapter, spiritual suffering is to be overcome by the expansion of the heart in the presence of the risen Christ.

Behind Jesus' victory over death was his willing and knowing laying down of life in response to the Father. This ecstatic movement is described in a natural metaphor in John 12:24. 'In all truth I tell you, unless a wheat grain falls into the earth and dies, it remains only a single grain; but if it dies it yields a rich harvest.' The context of this saying and its solemn beginning caution the reader against hasty interpretation.

As Passover is approaching, some Gentiles who come to worship at the festival express their desire to see Jesus. This tradition is carefully carried back to Jesus by his disciples. Now Gentiles as well as Jews are coming to him as they approach the Temple to worship. This news is for Jesus the signal of his Passion. 'Now the hour has come for the Son of man to be glorified' (12:23). Now he must fulfil his mission to draw all people to himself. On the cross he will be glorified as he reveals the Father's salvation to both Jew and Gentile; but this cannot happen unless he lays down his life, unless he yields his single human life to the ground of his Father's love. It is not just his message that yields a harvest (cf. Matt. 13:3ff) but the offering of his whole life. Without Jesus' laying down of his life for the sheep this saying would bear no sense at all for those who follow.

The saying about the wheat grain goes on, however. It is a hinge between talk of Jesus' death and talk of life for his disciples. It connects what we have already discussed with what we have yet to consider, the way to victory for those who come after Jesus. The saying continues,

> Anyone who loves his life loses it;
> anyone who hates his life in this world
> will keep it for eternal life.
> Whoever serves me, must follow me,
> and my servant will be with me wherever I am.
> If anyone serves me, my Father will honour him.
>
> (vv. 25–6)

So the saying about the wheat grain is also part of a choice Jesus gives between two ways of living. It reveals the fruitfulness of the way Jesus took, witnessed to in the fabric of creation itself,[6] to those who are looking for something beyond themselves and this world.

The saying points to a divine economy of life-through-death in which people are able to share through Jesus' self-offering and entirely by God's graciousness. The saying about the grain of wheat dying and the preceding verse about Christ's glorification make it clear that real, physical death is in view here; but the nature of Jesus' death and the verse following about discipleship make it equally clear that in the human case life does not automatically follow death. The grain of wheat stands for the whole human life which, body, mind and spirit, must be offered to God. Only because Christ's death was a willing and knowing offering to his Father could death be defeated. Only by sharing in that whole movement can Christ's victory be ours, when God honours those who follow in Christ's way of service. The striking phrase 'hating life in this world' makes it clear that no compromise is envisaged; letting go is a necessary condition to enter into life. So a person can either continue as a single grain, seeking security by grabbing at people and things and so remaining lost and alone as death comes, or he can decide to let go of life, his ego, and be kept safe by Christ within the eternal knowledge and love of God. As J.V. Taylor puts it, 'the choice for every human being is between death or death'.[7]

We shall not be able to let go with the same serenity as did Jesus because we are unfamiliar with the economy of love in which we participate. For Christ, death was the culmination

of a dying life, a life of complete commitment to love and
disregard for the ego. For those who follow, letting go will
feel like a putting to death of the person who has claimed
independence. This is quite a different matter from bargaining
with God – my letting go for God's life – it does not stop
physical death but will enable dying well.

> Who then devised the torment? Love.
> Love is the unfamiliar Name
> Behind the hands that wove
> The intolerable shirt of flame
> Which human power cannot remove.
>   We only live, only suspire
>   Consumed by either fire or fire.[8]

It would not be untoward to call 'letting go' an act of
heroism, taking as much courage as having the faith to hold
onto the ego that will inevitably be destroyed in the death of
the body;[9] but the struggle with self will be fruitful because
'in wrestling with our ambiguous passions we too can learn
to say "Into your hands I commit my spirit". Only in letting
ourselves enter that darkness will losing ourselves in God
become a possibility.'[10]

The terminally ill have a journey to make to a point of trust
in an unfamiliar Love lying beyond them. There may well be
a struggle to reach this point, but it would be quite wrong to
think of the struggle in itself as achieving meaning. When the
psychology of the situation is considered in isolation, this
can be the impression given. Bruce Rumbold, a Christian of
considerable pastoral experience, talks in his book *Helplessness
and Hope* of a 'religious dimension' which is 'integral' to terminal care.[11] What he says about letting go, however, makes
man the master of his fate: 'we must search within ourselves
for the meaning of our own lives, and struggle to reaffirm this
meaning in the face of death. The basis for hope is personally-
perceived meaning. This meaning may be expressed in, for
example, a Christian or an existentialist framework.'[12] Rumbold is trying to speak to as wide an audience as possible and

is also trying to avoid Christian dogmas being dished out by pastors as a palliative. Nonetheless, this cannot excuse language which, at the least, drives a wedge between talk of grace[13] from God's work for us in Christ and with us in the Holy Spirit: only correct understanding can feed correct practice.

The danger for too long has been that Christian identity in pastoral care be drowned in the sea of secular discipline uncritically adopted. The psychological level is important, but before addressing it we must be sure of the theological base on which it is founded. Without the living God there can be no eternal destiny for the psyche or any other human faculty. So we must pursue the question of how the human struggle to overcome the reality of death is related to the gracious invitation to life offered by God in Jesus Christ. Only then can we return to the psychological benefits of letting go.

More than Psychology

If the dying could construct an eternal identity out of their own struggling with their story there would have been no need for the Good Shepherd to lay down his life for the sheep and to lead them into pasture. As John 12:23ff makes plain, only the pattern of Christ's ecstasy can be victory over death for those who follow. John's Gospel is constantly directing the reader to the reality of God. Right from the beginning its aim is not to hem people into false hopes and dogmas but to reveal one central and utterly personal reality in which each human being may find total fulfilment, the eternal love of God. We have already seen how the cross was the culmination of a life of unbroken human communion with the Father. In his perfect human response Christ said yes to God on our behalf, securing humanity in the love which from the beginning the Father had for the son. The yes that the Father says to Jesus in the resurrection is now offered to the world, so that humankind is held between the ecstasy of the Father and the Son. A person can do nothing to achieve her own salvation, but must discover it as the truth of her being by accepting the call of

the Other to 'let go' of what she knows of herself so that she
might receive her true life from the Father.

> The lover knocked at the door of his beloved. 'Who
> knocks?' said the beloved from within. 'It is I,' said the
> lover. 'Go away. This house will not hold you and me.'
> The rejected lover went away into the desert. There he
> meditated for months on end, pondering the words of the
> beloved. Finally he returned and knocked at the door
> again.
>   'Who knocks?'
>   'It is you.'
> The door was immediately opened.[14]

Letting go is the way to discover that the renewed image,
our true spiritual self, comes from beyond: 'our person, our
"me", does not belong to us in our own right; we receive it
in the order of grace that perfects it. . . The deepest "I",
the element most personal and unique, is a *gift*'.[15]

Clearly much more is at stake here than a psychological
process, even one with an integral religious dimension. Each
person must be 'born again', completely transcending the old
existence (3:3ff). The fruitfulness of letting go is assured by
Christ's self-consecration to the Father, but the possibility of
letting go and its realisation in the lives of those who follow
Christ is the work of the Holy Spirit, who brings the truth of
Christ to the world (16:7). As Christ promised, he returns to
take his own to himself through the Spirit of truth (14:16f),
whom the Father sends at his request to stand by his disciples
in their weakness, dwelling in them and enabling a response
to him. The Spirit does not come to invade and destroy human
being but comes as a friend, another counsellor (14:16), who
in and through Jesus knows what it is like to dwell in human
nature. He penetrates a flesh already prepared by Jesus, in
order to bring the psycho-physical life of humankind into the
communion of God's own life (16:15).

The Holy Spirit comes to effect the wholesale renewal of
the image of God in us, of feelings and body as well as of soul
and reason. When the Spirit comes, the human spirit is raised

to new heights, the human heart is enlarged and a new identity is given which answers the bodily search for true love, as
the flesh finds its vocation as the place wherein the Holy Spirit
makes his dwelling.[16] As a patient responds in Christ to the
word which has been spoken to her she finds her whole self
to be grounded in the personal presence of one who takes her
outside the boundaries of her known self into Christ's own
eternal ecstasy in the Father. Though this movement has been
called deification or divinisation in classical theology it does
not comprise a drowning of humanity in a sea of divinity but
a union of love. To return to the picture in John 10, the sheep
grazing on pasture are fully satisfied but yet remain sheep.
Teilhard de Chardin expresses it in these words: 'the One is
so perfect that as it receives me and I lose myself in it I can
find in it the ultimate perfection of my own individuality'.[17]
Love waits for and respects the human search for ecstasy. He
neither ignores nor smothers human desire but purifies and
embraces it in the gift of adoption as a child of God.[18] T.S.
Eliot charts the way into the darkness:

> In order to possess what you do not possess
> You must go by the way of dispossession.
> In order to arrive at what you are not
> You must go through the way in which you are not.
> And what you do not know is the only thing you know
> And what you own is what you do not own
> And where you are is where you are not.[19]

There is no other true way to stand outside the self than to
abandon self-existence, the life of ego, and to find a new
identity in the call of Love. In the face of death more than a
reaffirmation of the past is needed. The past must be transcended in encounter with the living God. Letting go must
include a letting go of story, so that the story's subject is God,
who gathers up the fragments of past life and present suffering
into a meaningful whole. Simon Tugwell has it exactly right
when he says somewhere, 'We clutch at our little bits of truth
and force them into a pattern, when the key to the whole

puzzle is still missing. We make sense of our lives before our lives actually do make sense; we make sense of our friends, our families, even of our God, before we have known them and loved them to the end.' Only the act of unconditional trust takes us beyond all concepts, even the most fundamental ones, into personal truth. Fear of dispossession holds us back, but eros, the desire for completion, is not easily defeated.

The journey to a good and holy death need not be a smooth one. Defences abound behind which to retreat; yet great strides forward may also be taken, when insight is given and a response made. Moreover, every act of 'hating' self is part of one simple movement into darkness which has already been established once for all by Christ. His response as the only Son of the Father has been forged at the heart of humanity, to be realised in each person through faith. There is only one perfect ecstasy in which to share, Christ's Passion, and it is discovered in the darkness, when the hope for meaning is given up and the psyche laid down. Only by the letting go of egocentric stories, only by letting go of desire itself, can a sufferer become rooted in God and so in eternity.

Mary of Magdala's Story

The radical relationship between old and new life is clearly seen in the story of Mary of Magdala. In John's Gospel she first appears near the cross of Jesus at his crucifixion, with Jesus' mother and her sister, Mary the wife of Clopas (19:25). Her story continues in John 20. It is set 'on the first day of the week'. Whatever may be Mary's state of mind, it is the sabbath indeed. Christ is risen and there is a new day, a new creation. But it is still dark. Resurrection has not yet dawned upon a sleeping world: the good news has still to be revealed.

Mary comes to the tomb in the darkness, without true knowledge of Jesus Christ. This may seem a hard thing to say about one whom Christian tradition has identified with the 'sinner' who anointed Christ's feet, whose actions Jesus himself commended (Luke 7:37). And even though this identification is unwarranted, the story itself shows Mary to be one of Jesus' devoted and courageous followers. She goes far beyond the requirements of ritual mourning. Her weeping is an expression of a heart filled with love for a good man, now dead. She must go to be with her lord and master. It is the least she can do; it is all she can do.

Mary's story highlights an undeniable fact: religious faith need not help in the business of facing death. Faith itself must be judged. Of course Mary's situation is not ours – she had known Jesus in the flesh – but the fundamental blockage in understanding is not unlike ours. Her Jesus fits her human story. She sees him in human categories. He remains more the object of her devotion than the subject of her life. Thus, Jesus is *her* Lord, her supreme possession, but a possession nonetheless. For those who believe, faith has to be purged of this element of possessiveness. Believers, too, must meet Jesus through the darkness, as the One who acts beyond them. In Jesus' act Mary's ignorance is exposed. He is risen: while she looks in the tomb. Her story, even though Jesus is so central a figure in it, must be completely reshaped. The practical application of Mary's story, then, is much wider than those who believe. It applies to all who face death with a story which is constructed, because lived, around the ego. So it is worth pondering in more detail.

It is Mary's devotion to Jesus that takes her to the tomb. She does not expect to find hope there but consolation, a way of drawing back from the darkness of despair threatening to engulf her. She needs to tend to the dead body. In so doing she can hold on to the decaying certainty of the past and look towards the relief of her own death in the future. Dealing in death is easier than hoping. When she reaches the tomb she finds a stone rolled away and no body, and suddenly the ground is cut beneath her feet. Old certainties are undermined, consolation removed. The final chapter of her life with Jesus cannot be written. Jesus' resurrection takes away even that crumb of comfort. An empty tomb spells only disaster and causes her to panic. It is dawn on the first day of the week, but Mary is still in darkness, her devotion blinding her to the real meaning of events.

And yet – and yet the destruction of the old story is the beginning of the new. The new does not obliterate the old, but transcends it. Despair born out of ignorance holds Mary at the place where the risen Christ will appear. The sight which has destroyed old certainties and has taken away meagre consolation is also an invitation to question and discover hope afresh. The movement of weeping and stooping in grief becomes the movement of stooping and peering to face 'a vision of the absent One in his glory, represented by the angels.'[20] This is all to say that the destruction of the ego paves the way for God to act. The text does not allow us to see Christ's appearing as a process directly generated from despair. No, it is God's action from first to last. 'Woman, why are you weeping?', comes the question to Mary from God's messengers, as she faces the emptiness. Out of her despair comes this question and it has to be answered honestly, 'They have taken my Lord away, and I don't know where they have put him.'

Again the question comes, 'Why are you weeping?', this time from a stranger. Though she stands before the risen Christ himself, she fails to recognise him, forcing the features of Reality into the pattern of her expectation. The gardener – this must be the gardener. 'Who are you looking for?' Christ asks. Are you looking for the truth who is standing in front of you, for Life, a new story? Or will you continue to look for a way out of your pain and sorrow, a way of blunting the edges of a bitter end? Mary's answer shows her to be set on staying with her old story. 'Sir, if you have taken him away, tell me where you have put him, and I will go and remove him.' Then the Word speaks, into the depths of the obstinacy of the wounded heart: 'Mary!' His call pierces the darkness. Suddenly the light shines and despair is transformed into joy. Old questions have new answers: 'Why are you weeping?' Because I did not see. 'Who are you looking for?' The Jesus of my imagination.

In Mary's story we see so clearly the radical difference an

encounter with the living Word will make to a life. In their meeting we see Mary's need-driven devotion transformed by Christ's presence into complete personal fulfilment. The change starts in a moment, and though Mary still has much to learn ('Do not cling to me'), she is from that moment of meeting free and alive. If the story of one of Jesus' courageous and devoted followers includes so radical a transformation, might we not also expect those whose stories have been written outside Christian faith, whose conscious desire has been directed to objects other than Christ, to be utterly changed in their turning to the One who calls them? Old hopes will have to be destroyed and old securities abandoned in the light of Reality.

Mary's story makes it absolutely plain that the gift of faith is all God's. Christ himself is the only life-giver (6:33ff, 8:12, 11:25, 14:6). He is the one who calls beyond the darkness of suffering. Mary sees the Lord because he *chooses* to appear to her, honouring her search for him and her devotion, however misdirected. Involved in the discovery are Mary, Christ and two angels. As the text now runs, Peter and the beloved disciple make no contribution to Mary's search whatever. This is not to say that hope comes easily. The ground for their meeting is prepared through Jesus *not* appearing, through questions being asked and being met with silence and through Mary's descent into darkness as the last defences of the ego are stripped. Christ is risen; but his first gift to Mary is his absence, which paves the way for his making himself known.

The Escape from Ego

Nothing has been said that would devalue eros, the desire for self-transcendence; but eros cannot escape unchanged in an encounter with the living God: it must be enclosed, purified and transformed by God's own uncreated love, by agape.[21] Because eros can be bent back on itself to serve the needs of the ego, it can only be freed by the death of the ego. The ego may not be well formed. It may be dispersed, so to speak, in the *compulsive* service of others.[22] The death of ego should not be reduced to a moral level of understanding and equated with the ending of selfishness; it is the giving up of an existence which in any way seeks to secure itself in the created realm by any external act driven by a need for esteem, even acts of service. Eros must be realigned, returning to its origin in God's own fullness, where all is joy. 'Letting go', then, is the only way to find true meaning beyond the self. It leads to life because 'through ego-abandonment, the person becomes what he is, he finds himself the image of the self-abandoning God'.[23]

Struggle is very much a part of this movement out of ego. John uses both passive and active expressions to describe the way in to a new identity. A pair stand side by side in the Prologue:

> But to those who did *accept him*
> he gave power to become children of God,
> to those who *believed in his name*
> who were born not from human stock
> or human desire
> or human will
> but from God himself. (1:12)

Neither of these expressions preclude struggle; indeed, struggle is suggested by John's opposing of the cycle of desire and begetting with the gift of new birth from above. Both expressions suggest the necessity of a reconstruction of a person's story around the presence of Christ. The passive expression for faith of 'accepting him' points to the need to face painful realities. Christ, through his Spirit, brings the truth of human being (14:26). Each of the dying must face the clean pain of knowing their own nothingness before God. Without him no one is more than an isolated piece of the created order, like a single grain of wheat or shepherdless sheep. The active expression 'believing in him' represents the offering of the whole known self to Christ. Letting go starts from a movement of the will, a decision, but involves the whole heart, for true letting go is an act of love and unbounded commitment. A person has to accept that her life has its

source outside herself, outside the world even (15:19, 18:36).
She cannot be the lord of her life. She has to hand it over in
trust, hope and obedience to Another whose love does not
offer any easy answers in the midst of pain. The fruit of letting
go will be a new way of being, 'a condition of complete
simplicity', but one 'costing not less than everything'.[24]

The Prologue gives its readers more than a manner of
speaking in these phrases 'accepting him' and 'believing in
him'. The passivity of accepting and activity of believing
comprise part of the same single movement of joy, beyond
action and inaction, captured in Mary of Magdala's cry of
'Master!' and here also in a prayer of St Peter Canisius:

> I am not eager, bold
> Or strong – all that is past,
> I am ready not to do,
> At last, at last![25]

To translate John's terms into the language of spirituality,
this joy may be discovered in prayerful receptivity and surrender to Christ. There are patients who will say, 'I've tried
praying and it doesn't work'. They have used prayer as a
defence, as a way of bargaining to achieve an observable
result. Prayer 'works' when God is invited into the centre of
a patient's story, into the heart. This prayer allows the one
who offers it into the movement of Christ's self-consecration
for our sake. She is taken into all truth, which is an engagement with Love. The personal truth a pray-er meets will not
neatly round off her story; it will make it good by an act of
recreation. The dying person will be born again through
saying yes to the call of the One who has led her into darkness.
It would be unwise to tie this sort of praying down into words.
The words may be spoken by the pastor, with the patient's
Amen following,[26] or the patient may be able to take hold of
the name of Jesus. Certainly the movement of the Jesus prayer
– the indrawing of desire for God's Son and the outbreathing
of the old story to leave a naked self – is just what is necessary
to call down the joy of the anointing Spirit.[27]

We have not mapped out any tidy relationship between struggle and an encounter with God. God will act as and when he will; but it is humanly likely that the business of accepting the grace of Jesus Christ, in his absence or his presence, will involve a struggle with the demands of ego. Christ's voice, calling the patient to follow is, however, stronger. He calls his sheep from their enclosure into freedom, through the gate of his own self-offering. The command of Christ the King to follow him into suffering only makes things worse while we expect his call to make rational sense to us; but its meaning is given in the response it seeks. Trust *is* the sense of the call. There is no outside view to be had by anyone, not least by the one called. The meaning of vocation, then, is found in its fulfilment, that is, in obedience. In this obeying torment becomes the way of the cross. If the dying can give up the hope of mastering the darkness the way is open to their seeing the light shining within it. This is the vision of God described by mystics such as the thirteenth-century Franciscan Raymón Lull:

> Far above love is the Beloved; far beneath it is the Lover; and Love, which lies between these two, makes the Beloved to descend to the Lover and the Lover to rise toward the Beloved. And this ascending and descending is the being and the life of Love – of that Love which makes the Lover endure pain and which ever serves the Beloved.[28]

The pattern of the new life of the Spirit transcends all psychology. It is not crucifixion without resurrection (a descending only), nor resurrection without crucifixion (an ascending only), but a being *held* in the Love of God within the pain, in obedience, with human love encompassed from above and beneath, transcended and fulfilled by a life that has never been overcome by the darkness, by a Love which is stronger even than death.

Eternal Life and the End of Suffering

Since beginning to state the benefits of letting go, we have taken a long detour to highlight the inadequacy of purely psychological understanding of the search for meaning in the face of death. In the course of it we have established that those who encounter Christ with an open heart receive a new story which transcends the old. Eternal life is new life, a gift from God through Jesus Christ, which cannot be attained simply by a reaffirmation of past values. This is not, however, to extract the movement from the ego into God from the realm of the psyche. True, the mystery of human being is fulfilled 'from above', it cannot be grasped; but a patient who is born of the Spirit will know it, as one who has received a new identity as a child of God.

With a new story and identity comes knowledge of God, which is the truth enabling a person to transcend the need to exist. The only definition of eternal life in John's Gospel is made in terms of knowledge: 'And eternal life is this: to know you, the only true God, and Jesus Christ whom you have sent' (17:3). As we have said, it is not possible to take an outside rational view of 'the meaning of suffering', but there is a tacit knowing to be had, beyond passive observation or active conceptualisation, in the movement of letting go. In filial obedience to the Father 'responsive creativity finds what it has to say only through the saying of it, and discovers the greatness of what it celebrates only through the celebration of it'.[29] The knowledge is of an intensely personal nature, the joining of hearts in a shared story. In this knowing and being known the barriers between persons are broken, leaving a oneness which is intensely affirming. Those who do obey Christ's call find that they belong to his Passion. No closer to their true home can they be than when opening their arms wide upon the cross of their own suffering, where Christ's ecstasy upholds and enjoins theirs:

> Love, Love, O Love, thy touch so quickens me,
>   Love, Love, O Love, I am no longer I:

> Love, Love, O Love, thyself so utterly
> Thou giv'st me, Jesu, that I can but die.[30]

To be no longer by oneself – more than that, to be no longer oneself, is, at one and the same time, to die and to live. It is the coincidence of ecstasy and death. The past dies by being renewed for eternity. The single self has fallen to the ground; the harvest has begun. The loneliness of the terminally ill can be 'treated' within the hospice community by the opportunity it brings to belong, but the 'cure' to inner loneliness, the cry of the heart, is given finally by the presence of God speaking within and beyond community (16:33). God's presence never answers the question, 'Why me?' at face value, but the question is not meant at face value.[31] Rather, the question is undermined by God's personal presence saying, 'Why ever you are suffering, your human life is accepted, affirmed and loved in Christ, and therefore your human potential is fulfilled. I am your Friend'.[32] Those who listen to his voice will no longer suffer spiritually, because their hearts will be filled with Love. Their search for meaning will be over, because 'when a person loves, all that is in his power is invested with a sense of purpose, as available for the other, or becomes a cause or occasion of gratitude, as received by gift from the other.'[33] Those who listen to God's voice will know the truth, which is an eternal and personal reality of unconditional love around and within, enabling them to transcend self-existence. They will know the truth and the truth will know them. With God with them and in them (14:17) they will be able to step into the darkness willingly and knowingly.

It is far from easy for most to acknowledge their growing dependence on others, allied as it is to a sense of shame; but in the new life of the Spirit a new dignity is given, a dependence on God, which brings strength rather than weakness (8:14). Every child of God will be helped to go forward willingly, because 'once I experience that, for God, I represent a good and a You, I can then put full confidence in the gift of being and freedom presented to me, and coaffirm myself as really affirmed from all eternity'.[34] This is the knowing assurance of seeing the self as both being nothing and being loved, an assurance expressed in doxology in the Prologue of John's Gospel (esp. 1:16). It is an assurance that grows in a spiral of faith, because those who serve Christ by following him are honoured by the Father (12:25). Many who make a small act of trust find that feelings of peace and security follow. Despite the total threat of death, a total hope is at hand in the unconditional love of God, enabling a patient to eye herself with a certain detachment and to take her growing incapacity and loss of control less seriously.[35]

The total hope of Christ is a gift that breaks gently into life, like a smile. It does not satisfy reasonable expectations, hopes for earthly happiness or self-preservation. Human beings are not by nature immortal, but when they are divinised hopes for some kind of future are fulfilled in a present trust in the One who calls from beyond, yet within, a person's story. The growth of a trusting attitude to the future is the most basic expression of hope. When Christ calls in the face of death he bids his followers to trust God and not to let their hearts be troubled (14:1). We are involved here in different aspects of the one practice of hoping; a change in self-understanding, a change in willing and a change in feeling.[36] All are signs that through obedience to Christ's call to follow a person has found a final orientation in the darkness, where light shines: 'Light comes from up there, it comes from something stretching above me, something transcending me, something preceding me.'[37] Knowingly, willingly and trustingly a person can die like Christ, in total hope, sharing in his freedom to lay down his life in ecstasy.

My exploration of the psychological aspects of letting go should not detract from the simplicity of the movement itself. As Matthew Fox says, 'the joy of ecstasy . . . is a non-elitist spirituality. . . It is a spirituality as if people mattered'.[38] The offer of eternal life is open to all people – the Samaritan outcast, the learned religious, the fisherman. I had the privilege to witness Don's discovery of the truth.

Don came to the hospice angry that he had been cheated of time.[39] He was full of existential guilt and kept asking to be forgiven. After a talk with a chaplain, however, he said to her, 'There's light now

between me and Jesus. Can you see it?' Don's silent witness to the call
of Love was to let go. Nobody noticed – the hospice routine of 'all care
given' closed in around his body and few would have guessed the inner
journey that Don had already made to peace and eternity in Christ. The
last time I went to visit him he was sleeping, and it was clear that,
though not physically dead, Don had died to the self that had been full
of worry and guilt. Now he enjoyed true freedom of spirit, and it did
not matter that a night remained before he was to reach the end of his
mortality.

I said to the man who stood at the gate of the year, 'Give
me a light that I may tread safely into the unknown.'
And he replied, 'Go out into the darkness and put your
hand into the hand of God. That shall be to you better
than light and safer than a known way!' So I went forth
and finding the Hand of God, trod gladly into the night.
And he led me towards the hills and the breaking of day
in the lone East.[40]

6

JUDGEMENT

The judgement of women and men by God is not an idea that carers readily accept. They think that 'judgement' is what God does to the dead, to punish the souls of helpless patients for their wrongdoing or for their lack of religious faith. If God is just, and not a monster, they argue, then the only possible thing for him to do would be to offer sufferers the compensation of eternal bliss. God could not care any less for them than those who love and care for them on earth. Judgement appears the very antithesis of unconditional love.

If God did gratuitously punish people, as some imagine, then there would indeed be an issue of justice to deal with; but he does not. We see this clearly in John's Gospel, which removes even the language of retribution employed in the other Gospels and in the Pauline epistles. In it, God sends his Son into the world not to condemn the world but to stand before the world as a beacon in the darkness, to enlighten everyone by revealing the truth of their lives, who is the Father. God sends Jesus out of love so that all people might see him as their truth; and his love judges the human heart. The condemnation that carers fear is not something which God imposes on the undeserving 'from above'; only grace and truth come from that direction! The Gospel tells us that punishment is self-inflicted: evildoers shrink from the light for fear of being exposed and in so doing forfeit the grace of knowing God (3:16ff).

On the contrary, Jesus' mission lends unconditional value to the life of each individual in the sight of God, because human life can have no eternal value unless it is judged by a personal and eternal standard of love outside itself. The boundedness of life by death gives life a quality and a poignancy without which it would not be recognisably human, but if that bounded life is a mere chasing after the wind, it is futile. On the other hand, for a human life to have an ultimate meaning it cannot be judged in an arbitrary way. There cannot be some hidden criterion by which an alien God sets upon us. Because an absence of vindictiveness in judgement does not automatically guarantee compassion, we must discover that the judgement of God is given in the Word made flesh, a *human* divinity, in his meeting with sinners.

This chapter makes a sustained attempt to tell of the love of God and the freedom it makes for human destiny. It starts with a meditation on the compassion of Jesus for sinners, which protects them from accusation and gives them the space to choose to obey his word. The decision for or against the love of God offered in Jesus comprises God's judgement. Though Jesus is now no longer physically present, faith in his word still brings freedom to the dying. Even partial faith will lead a patient from darkness into light. Every pastor is present to witness to the truth, to follow God in word and deed in the way of unconditional love, to rejoice in signs of truth being received and to suffer with Christ in the face of despair. Above all, pastors should be aware of the limits of their responsibility: it is God's purpose to save, their job to trust the one who condemns no one.

Guilt and the Grace of God

There is no other story on the theme of judgement more worthy of attention than the independent tradition which most editions of the New Testament locate at John 7:53–8:11, the story of the woman taken in adultery. Its vocabulary is Lukan and, indeed, some witnesses place it after Luke 21:38; yet it finds a ready home within the ethos and theology of John's Gospel.

The following exposition does not deny the historical character of the incident but draws out a spiritual meaning by taking the voices of the scribes and Pharisees as 'accusers'.

This approach opens out the text to the situation where no one is physically present to confront the sinner with his failure to walk rightly in the fullness of life. Anyone dying under a weight of sin, therefore, is covered by this reading. This weight may show itself in many ways, including fear, sorrow, anger, lassitude, uncommunicativeness and guilt. An internal reading of the accusers is particularly pertinent to those who *feel* guilty, as it covers not only the fact that people have sinned but also the particular case where, as Freudian theory has it, internalised parental prohibitions and social mores rise up to accuse. While guilt feelings are not necessarily a symptom of sin, they may well be present and must be dealt with within the whole process of recentring the patient's story around the presence of Jesus, which is the judgement of the ego.

In John 8 accusers come to Jesus looking to him to seal their condemnation of a sinner. In their eyes she is a category, one of many 'women of this kind', hardly a person at all. There is no doubt that she is guilty. She has been caught in the very act of adultery, a sin punishable by death. Her actions lead her to public exposure and a state of complete vulnerability. Accusing voices are raised against her, sounding out a cold morality that seeks to compromise Jesus. If he should seek to contradict them, he will appear lax and unconcerned with the right and good.

Jesus condemns no one: he judges, offering freedom from death. His judgement, when it comes, is first directed to the accusers. It comes from a discerning silence and a humility which avoids even a loving turning to the victim of guilt. As morality rears its head, Jesus bends down to write. He is close to the earth, in touch with the weakness of his own humanity, and so in touch with the strength of his heavenly Father, as the voices continue to press in. When he sits up to face the accusers it is with a true uprightness which stems from humility. In one sentence Christ sows the seed of peace: 'Let the one among you who is guiltless be the first to throw a stone at her.' His word seeks neither to trick nor to condemn but to reveal the truth of human pride and weakness. Then he returns to silence and the honesty of the earth while the truth does its work. The voices, humbled by their being shown the deceitfulness of their demands, withdraw from the scene. The woman is left alone in the presence of Jesus. As Augustine so aptly put it, 'there remains a great misery [miseria] and a greaty pity [misericordia].'

Jesus straightens but remains in his seat, continuing to teach the true meaning of judgement. He is in no way lax in his dealings with her, but his is an uprightness of love which holds the bright ideals of the Law within a more brilliant cherishing of human frailty: 'Woman,' – he addresses her personally, as he might his own mother – 'where are they? Has no one condemned you?' In the light of Jesus no human standard has the power to condemn. Condemnation only comes to those who reject the Light, wishing to avoid the exposure of their true nature. Thus, in the light of Jesus, the accusers' proud way of self-perfection is exposed as, in truth, unattainable. Only Jesus, who remains without sin by his perfect listening and obedience to the Father, can judge and save. He invites the woman to see her acquittal in the stilling of the voices of accusation and, critically, in his own accept- ance of her: 'Neither do I condemn you'.

This is forgiveness: a new life made possible by a meeting with Jesus Christ. The woman is only free from the threat of death because he alone has spoken for her. But his speaking is her judgement. What will this woman do with her life? The voices which sought to exploit her weakness and which demanded death are now replaced by the one voice of truth, who in speaking to her gives her back human dignity and bids her be truly free: 'Go away,' – go from this place of accusation and exposure – 'and from this moment sin no more.' The woman will still die one day, but she will always be free if she accepts this word to her. It is not a command to desist from a particular act, but a personal call to begin a wholly new way of life focussed entirely on her meeting with Jesus and his gift of forgiveness. This word cannot be grasped by the ego in its quest for moral security, because Jesus' demand is far stricter than her accusers'. It can be accepted only in the key in which it is spoken, as a word of love which knows what is possible in response to love. The going Jesus invites by his word is a movement of joy and thanksgiving for the gift of being utterly and undeservedly loved.

The deepest meaning of this encounter with Jesus is not that accusing voices are stilled and the past disposed of but that the truth is revealed and the past redeemed. The way ahead is now illumined by a love for which sin was searching in self-destructive and self-deluding ways. The enfleshed word of Jesus conveys the gift of human, unadulterated love to one seeking it. Now the woman can see her glory in Jesus and is without excuse. If she refuses the way he opens, then there lies her condemnation; if she accepts it, she receives true life, which is the freedom to live eternally in the movement from Jesus to his Father.

Judgement and Witness in John's Gospel and Now

One of the un-Johannine aspects of John 7:53ff is that judgement is not mediated by revelation, that is, by Jesus' witness to himself and his Father. In John, those who meet Jesus must make a decision to receive his testimony or to remain wilfully in an ignorance of their own construction. This is the import of the confrontation between Jesus and the Jews in John 8: the Jews ignore his revelation because their identity is threatened. These pious men were not prepared to be directed by Jesus beyond their secure image of the historical Abraham to the eternal truth shared by the Father and the Son from the beginning. They tried to overcome him because they would not comprehend him (1:5).

Others who had met Jesus, on the other hand, were moved by grace gradually from their position of ignorance towards the light, people like Nicodemus and the Samaritan woman. Those who were drawn to Jesus were drawn to him not because his claims for God and himself were self-evidently true but because the truth of God which he revealed in himself and by his words showed them the truth of their own lives. This is what John means in verse 9 of the Prologue when he says that Jesus was the true light that gives light to everyone. He is the answer to the deepest searchings, hopes and aspirations of humanity. This is suggested by the way that belief is illuminated in vivid human metaphors. Those who are saved will never thirst again and their hunger will be satisfied.[1]

John knows of no abstract concept of judgement outside this decision for or against Jesus. Those who accept the truth of Jesus, however partially, have faith. Faith, for John, is primarily a question of being willing to receive Jesus as the One whom he reveals himself to be, the One from the Father for us. The underlying character of *this* faith is one of personal relationship with a Word who is 'in fact the true source and centre of all that exists and its presence requires the abandonment of the whole enterprise of understanding and managing the world from a centre in a human ego'.[2] The claims Jesus makes are not supposed to be held in the mind as faith: they are signs drawing Jesus' hearers towards a true contemplation of God, as the Gospel makes plain: 'I am the bread of life' is both an invitation to eat and a promise of satisfaction to those whose life contemplating their own ego has left them wanting. Contemplation is a unified act of the whole person in which the mind is fully given to the heart's truth; it is the scholar's folly to siphon off from personal faith a 'rational' or 'intellectual' component.

The claims of Jesus, which have a real and substantial personal content, are also pillars of shared vision around which the true community of Jesus is formed by the Holy Spirit. In the cosmic battle between the prince of this world and Jesus Christ he must be known as he is by his disciples. The Gospel is written both to nourish and protect the life of the community of faith. As it says in chapter 20, 'Those [signs] written here have been recorded in order that you [plural] may believe that Jesus is the Christ, the Son of God, and that through this faith you [plural] may have life by his name.' The community of faith is the place where truth is proclaimed and lived out in its fullness, where Christ is glorified in the common life.[3] Within the fullness of community, however, the Gospel gives licence to, indeed approves of, a variety of responses to Jesus Christ from all types of humanity, some halting and partial.

All this argument gives value to those who, in this secular-

ised age, have had little or no contact with the Christian
tradition. We need not lose hope if those whose minds are
clouded by illness and pain fail to grasp the *form* of Jesus'
claims in scripture, and still less those of his followers in
doctrine. The crucial aspect is the movement into which
Christ's words draw the reader. In John, Christ speaks not
as a god but as the Son of God who is truly human, one who
does not guard his ego but who receives his being from the
Father. When Jesus speaks of himself, therefore, he points
beyond himself to his Father, a relationship into which the
listener is invited.[4] The truth of God is held within two
relationships: the relationship of the human Jesus with his
Father and the relationship of the human Jesus with those he
meets. We may hope that in the community of service formed
around patients in a hospice Christ may draw others to himself and to his Father through the humanity of his friends.[5]

The Place of the Pastor

It is not for the disciples of Jesus to condemn: they are to
witness, to draw people to the only Son of the Father. Their
witness is championed by the Paraclete who comes precisely to
show that the world is wrong about sin, justice and judgement
(16:8). In his strength Jesus' friends stand by the dying to
overturn conceptions which are man-made and conveniently
marginal to the business of being human by a personal call
to faith in Jesus leading to eternal life and freedom. This they
do by following the pattern of John the Baptist, the first
witness, who threw the attention of his followers beyond himself, saying, 'Look! This is the one' (1:15). Rather than having
to use many words on behalf of an absentee God, a disciple
of Jesus has only to point to the Word made flesh (1:39), by
being present as a human being who knows Jesus personally
and through him knows God as a gracious Father.

There are times when it would be better not to talk of Jesus,
as Jesus-language is not always effectual or productive. I was
talking to an educated middle-class woman who gave me the
impression of wanting to be in control. She engaged me in

conversation, taking as a subject my obvious interest in religion.

Jean: What do you think Jesus was doing between the ages of 12 and 20?

RR: I've no idea. Riding his motorbike, I suppose!

Jean: I've been reading this book which suggests that he was living with the Essenes. This chap had access to the Dead Sea Scrolls. You've heard of them, haven't you?

Whether Christ is named or not, at all times humility should be the mode and love be the motive by which we speak, because religious language can be so easily used by both parties as a defence, a way of feeding the needs of the ego. Christ is present. We are part of a team. We are present as a friend to the dying, much more ready to listen to them and to God than to speak from a package of truth that sets us apart and protects us from the rest of humanity. The danger is that we use people's fears and weakness to manipulate them, rather than helping people to let go into the love of God and to die well. The only way to avoid this is to be human and to be aware of our own needs and fears as well as those of the patient, to wait as equals and friends for the Word to speak. John Austin Baker says, 'the challenge to Christians is to make something of the essence of their hope and joy available through the data of the human situation'.[6] The fact that God supremely reveals himself in the incarnation shows that this is not only a possible way of communicating the truth but the supreme way. 'Our work is to follow his leading, to be available and approachable and to learn that truth is so often in a relationship rather than in words'.[7]

I was privileged to play a small part in Don's journey into faith, though Don saw 'light between himself and Jesus', as he put it, only after he had spoken with the chaplain. Here is part of a conversation we had which I feel was significant, maybe because it started from Don's weakness. As I sat holding his hand I tried to discern his need and to answer it with talk of grace.

RR: What are you looking for?

Don: Peace. Security.

RR: I've found peace.

Don: Are you married?

RR: Yes; but I didn't find it there.
Silence.
RR: It was given to me – a present!
Don: That's nice.
RR: (later in the conversation) I'm glad to be here.
Don: I'm glad you're here. Thank you for your spirit.

Christians are not afraid to be agents of God's judgement because they know for themselves that judgement is not God's 'no' to a human story, even to any part of it. Quite the contrary: no human story can be made whole until its darker themes are met by tenderness. Edwin Muir's poem, 'The Strange Return', has a man facing his past, trying to

> Make friends with evils, take his part,
> Salute the inner and outer strife,
> The bickering between doubt and faith,
> Inherit the tangle he had left,
> Outface the trembling at his heart.[8]

This is the life which the Word must enlighten and by no means deny. This is possible because he speaks to the heart of life from silence and eternity, outside the tangle and the trembling. From the beginning his life has been the light of all humanity. He needs only to be recognised as the One who comes from without, who brings the true life of self. Muir's poem continues and ends as the man sees that by him

> Three feet away a little tree
> Put out in pain a single bud
> That did not fear the ultimate fire
> And in a flash he knew it all,
> The long-forgotten and new desire,
> And looked and saw the tree was good.

As was said at the beginning, Christ is no foreign standard. He wills to be seen as the One who offers life, reaching out in love and in solidarity with the pain of being human. Christ is not present to put human existence to waste but to envelop it in grace and truth and offer it to the Father. He makes each story whole by answering the human search for love with the Holy Spirit who brings people to new birth as children of God. The Holy Spirit it is who gives grace of crucifixion to those facing death, because Christ's judgement is not a glossing over story, nor even seeing the story in a new light, but is a dying to a life lived from the ego, so that the story is remade, open, but strangely familiar. The final, fully human story of each child of God is joined to the one eternal story of the uniquely loved Son. This means that nothing can be wasted: everything finds fulfilment in *his* 'It is finished!' from the cross. Human need is met by God flinging open his own life and drawing people into it, giving them knowledge of who he is in himself, Love. As the Fathers said in awe, it is not that God has made a part of himself known, but that we know in part who he is in himself.[9] The whole origin and destiny of those made in the image of God is a participation by grace in the very life of the Trinity.

Joy, Sorrow and Pastoral Responsibility

The previous chapter ended with a picture of a man who knew Life before he died. Pastors do not witness because of the results they achieve or even because God achieves results through them; they witness because in obeying Christ's command his joy is fulfilled in them. Nonetheless, being as human as patients' relatives, they will hope for a sign of victory over death. Words may be said by the patient which indicate the work of God within, perhaps the most significant being those expressing gratitude or sorrow to the pastor after prayer. The incarnation means, however, that the truth has been expressed most profoundly in the flesh rather than in statements of belief; it must also be received in the flesh, in personal encounter: 'In all truth I tell you, whoever welcomes the one I send, welcomes me, and whoever welcomes me welcomes the one who sent me' (John 13:20). As Cicely Saunders says, 'people are not always so far away from faith as we think. Light does come, I believe very often, though we may have to recognise it by seeing "signs following" rather than by hearing explicit verbal confessions of faith'.[10]

It takes some discernment to read the signs of faith. Those who hear Christ's voice will bear the mark of freedom, but this freedom may express itself unexpectedly, for example, in protest against God or the world.[11] Depression and fear will be displaced by a basic trust in the One who calls them by name and who also cares for those they are leaving in the world. They will, then, become able to release their family from the grip of their expectations, while looking outward in love to their needs and beyond to the needs of nursing staff and neighbours. Above all, they will show themselves thankful for the gift of their life.

Kathleen had a rotting breast which leaked and which stank without extensive and frequent treatment. When her husband was dying a couple of years earlier she decided not to undergo surgery as she did not want to worry him or live on after him. After his death she discovered that there was still life left for her to enjoy. She always seemed cheery, to my knowledge never complaining about her condition, and concerned for all those around. I never asked what she thought about Jesus.

The ability of some to transcend their suffering, with all the joy which attends it, brings us back to the dark side of judgement. We see that 'natural life is but the sub-structure for a life of communion with God'.[12] To miss that high vocation of sharing in God's eternal love and to finish life alone, empty and afraid, as a creature out of communion with his creator, is a profound tragedy, one which is only heightened by a catholic understanding of the scope of Christ's incarnation, death and resurrection. By his life of loving obedience he wins forgiveness for all. Now risen, he stands alongside humanity as a friend offering his support to our search for meaning in the face of death. The response he invites is a simple one, one which he has already made possible for our sake, comprising the letting go of ego in order to receive the gift of self beyond ourselves. This is evangelical repentance, a response to grace.[13] There is no God-made barrier between time and eternity, death and life, mortality and adoption as God's child. We can, even in our weakness and impotence, respond in Christ to the call of love.

Pastors play their part in Christ's ministry of judgement
not so much by what they say but by their experience of
grace. They know that, while they share fully in human weakness, they have been forgiven. They do not condemn (3:17);
by their awareness of sin and grace they hold the mirror of
self-knowledge to the face of those they meet. In John 20, the
disciples are sent out to minister pardon through their sharing
in Jesus' breath. His Spirit leads them into truth, the knowledge that the wounds of Christ, and their own wounds in his,
are the way to salvation. Far from condemning the vulnerable
for specific offences, pastors will be able to convey to them
the felicity of sin, in so far as it brings them out of the crowd
before the judgement of God. The presence of someone who
knows a way out of 'the cavern of sin'[14] is vital for healing.
'Being there' is not enough. Pastoral responsibility entails
speaking the truth in a way which addresses the whole of
another's life with tenderness.[15] Humbly, pastors offer through
embodied care the hands and side of the risen Lord.

Yet many people cannot respond to Christ, trapped by their
past choices and way of living. For them what started as self-
love has shaded into self-hatred. They wilfully reject what is
good and true because they despise it. This is why John sees
the judgement falling on those who practise evil, on those who
do not want the light of God to expose the true nature of
their actions (3:20). Jesus does not condemn (3:17) but his
judgement is to reveal the truth of everyone, as a varnish
shows up the grain of wood or litmus the acidity of liquid.
The Father, understanding human weakness because he has
known it through his Son, calls gently to the dying person so
that he does not abuse the dignity of his creature, and so that
this beloved creature is free to say yes to his call of grace or
to say no. There cannot be one possibility without the other.
For those who refuse it, the call of love is a word of condemnation, for to let go of their ego would be to let go of all they
claim for themselves. They are left with all that a creature
has by right, which is nothingness, death.

Philip Larkin, whose own life was overshadowed by the
power of death, gives in his poem 'Deep Analysis' an agonising
voice to the bewilderment of eros denied by ego. The voice of

eros questions ego as to why he had not been true to his deepest desire for love, why his striving and pride and fear had shut her out and left her, so

That my own heart drifts and cries, having no death
Because of the darkness,
Having only your grief under my mouth
Because of the darkness.[16]

This is a condemnation which cannot be ignored simply because it is human self-condemnation. All of us would like to deny this reality, but the truth is that in every sphere, divine and human, love allows both freedom and suffering.

The staff managed to nurse a delirious man into a conscious enough state to be able to refuse the soup that was 'good for him'. He made the choice not to drink it, becoming angry when they tried to feed it to him. He could even have refused his pain-killers. This assertion of independence is a tribute to health care. But maintaining human dignity has a cost: people can turn away from what holds them in health or being.

Because God *is* love there cannot be a trick up his sleeve by which he can surreptitiously overcome the free choice of his creatures. His love is both the means to life and the end of life; and there is no one, divine or human, who can coerce in love. As Canon W.H. Vanstone has remarked, 'The external restraint which love practices is often a mark of its freedom from internal limit.'[17]

Carers are right to think that a God of love would not condemn his creatures: condemnation comes from a refusal to accept God's acceptance of us and the painful enlightenment it brings to our condition. God can indeed satisfy the deepest thirst and hunger of eros for union, beauty and truth, but only if there is a movement of grace from the false ego to the true 'I am'. The pastors' responsibility is to enter into that movement of grace, to be there to love to the uttermost those for whom Christ gave up his life, hugging the contours of unconditional love, by the measure of which all are judged. They must trust God, respecting love's limits and sharing its pain, knowing that in doing this they share in the judgement of Jesus. The Lord himself offered a morsel of food to Judas at the Last Supper (13:26). It was a sign of hospitality, maybe even one giving special honour to his guest. No greater love could have been shown nor greater opportunity for repentance given. Judas took the morsel but spurned Jesus in his heart, making room there for Satan to enter in. Though all the while Jesus knew what was in the man, he let him step into the night.

The way of the cross is never easy, but the simplicity of movement is staggeringly simple, a laying down of life in the pattern of Jesus. Though witnesses do this out of faithfulness and to give glory to God they may take comfort that the love of Christ freely offered did and does change the whole course of the lives of many. To the extent to which pastors and all those in the hospice community witness to that love, so there is real hope, even for those whose lives have become despairing and fragmented, that they will find themselves called into light.

> I found him nearest when I missed him most;
> I found him in my heart, a life in frost,
> A light I knew not until my soul was dark.[18]

THE GLORY OF GOD AND THE SALVATION OF THE WORLD

Readers of this book have followed the journey described in Chapter 1, from time to eternity, in two different ways. Chapters 2 and 3 covered it from the perspective of the pastor, charting the attitudes and actions necessary for the making of eternal communion. Chapters 4 and 5 tracked the path to victory which a patient needs to make with Christ through the Holy Spirit in order to die well. Chapter 6 took a step back to survey the meeting between pastor and patient, tackling the issue of how it contributes to Christ's loving judgement of the terminally ill. We now end the journey by taking another, final step back, returning to the perspective of the first chapter, though using a more particular vocabulary, the language of glory.

It is good to do this for three reasons. First, the pleasure and end of exploration, as T.S. Eliot reminds us, is 'to arrive where we started and know the place for the first time'.[1] Second, integrity demands a return to a level beyond the personal. If this author is to avoid a fault of which he accuses others, of using theology to serve secular assumptions about human need, then further detachment from need is necessary to bring awareness of God and his glory beyond immediate issues of care. Third, glory is John's perspective from first to last, to which it is good to be true in a book claiming Johannine spirituality as its source. As the Prologue proclaims,

> . . . and light shines in darkness
> and darkness could not overpower it.

> The Word became flesh,
> he lived among us,
> and we saw his glory,
> the glory that he has from the Father
>   as only Son of the Father,
> full of grace and truth. (vv. 5,14)

We shall soon find that this concentration on truth for true love's sake provides a further, prophetic dimension to pastoral care of the dying. Not rushing ahead to the conclusion, however, provides a chance to be with Jesus in his self-consecration to God's truth as he faces his coming hour of crucifixion and death. The story is told in the seventeenth chapter of the Gospel.

Protection and Purpose in the Truth

Jesus, lifting his eyes to his true home in heaven, asks his Father to glorify him, at the hour of his death. Throughout his ministry he has been revealing the Father's glory; but now, as the hour has come when he is to be lifted up on the cross, Jesus asks his Father to give him the glory due to a Son. He has completed the work that he has been given to do by the Father; now it must bear fruit in a final, boundless act of love. The glory of God will be revealed when the One sent by the Father is exalted in triumph on his way back to heaven. On the cross, enthroned for all time as king, he will be given power to gather his own to himself and to judge the world for its refusal to accept his service.

Even before his arrest and trial by men, Jesus has conquered the world. He willingly drinks from his Father's cup of suffering for the sake of his own. Through prayer, in the face of impending danger, Jesus is glorified as he gives himself completely to the Father. His humanity, rather than standing in the way of divine love, brings immense fruitfulness as it falls to the ground and dies. In Christ, the love of God is able, as it would not otherwise have been able, to embrace and transfigure human flesh. Jesus' glorification is the honouring of his human trust, obedience and knowledge by the Father's divine majesty, authority and power. It happens through a loving, personal exchange of attributes. The gift of divine glory, which has always been the Son's by right from the beginning, is received personally on behalf of humanity by the Son, through his total offering of himself to the Father. The cross is the precise way by which the Son can love the Father without limit, and so find a dwelling place for human nature within the fullness of divine life. God's glory is freely given to Jesus, as he requests it, so that whoever believes in him should not perish but have everlasting life.

On the cross the glory of God does far more than enfold the suffering flesh of Jesus from without, raising him above pain and anguish; it shines out of his suffering, from within the darkness which he has freely chosen and taken into himself, so that life can be revealed to those who receive him in their suffering. Christ glorifies the Father as the Father glorifies him by bringing the Father's salvation to light. Jesus' disciples have known the true God. They have obeyed the Father's command to listen to his beloved Son. They have received the word he has sent in Jesus and seen the Father in him and his works. But now the evil one threatens: the news of his departure has left the disciples troubled and in danger of losing faith. Christ prays that, in his absence, God himself will protect the flock. The Father will glorify the Son by receiving him into his heavenly home and by sending the Spirit in his name. He will bring the presence of the risen Christ to them and recall to them the truth of all their Lord has said. The glory of the cross does not flood the world's stage with light but offers in Christ's flesh a point of pure brilliance, of absolute embodied truth, which is carried by the Holy Spirit deep into the hearts of those who remain searching for a way in a world that remains in darkness.

Jesus' prayer wins for the disciples joy in the face of suffering and evil. In the Spirit, they are given a share in the oneness of the Father and the Son which has withstood everything. Without Christ they can do nothing: but within him they too are assured of his victory. The cross becomes the place where suffering can be met and overcome, where each disciple can be lifted up by Jesus and taken to the Father. Christ did not suffer alone and neither will the disciples: the Father will be with them and in them, because he loves them in the Son and, with the Son, is present in the Spirit. He waits to receive the gift of their trusting, obeying and serving love as they face their hour, so that the Son and the Father may be glorified in them.

The witness of Christ opens the door for the witness of his disciples. The Father and the Son are glorified when, in the power of the Spirit, the humanity of Jesus' disciples becomes ever more translucent to the love of God. Their humanity can be perfected in love as his was, through their offering made in and through him. Christ the Good Shepherd dies for the sheep to protect the flock; the grain of wheat falls into the ground to yield the harvest: but the flock can be added to and the crop increase, if the sheep who follow Christ are faithful and the harvest-grain falls freely. That is why Jesus' parting prayer is that his disciples may be one as he and his Father are one; for it is only by sharing the divine life themselves that the disciples have anything true to share with others. The glory of the cross is that it is the throne from which the crucified Son and the crucifying Father[2] offer for all time their oneness in the Spirit; in God's glory, which the darkness has never overcome, the children of God can continue to bear and reveal in their communion the fruit of divine love.

The Necessity of Death

John is of all the evangelists the most daring; it is he who identifies so unflinchingly the glory of God with the crucifixion of the Son of Man. All hours of Jesus' life lead to his one hour of exaltation (2:4; 7:6; 12:27). John is giving something other than a religious interpretation to a universal truth. Professor John Bowker argues that death is, anyway, life yielding *for* life, a 'sacrifice' so to speak, which religious traditions describe with varying degrees of accuracy: 'it is not possible to have life on any other terms than those of death; but where you *do* have death, there immediately you have the possibility of life'.[3] This may well be a correct cosmological principle, but it is not one which John adumbrates by having Jesus die as the Lamb of God. John is interested in the gift of eternal life by grace, not in the natural ebb and flow of universal existence. He is making the hiatus of death on a cross the very point at which the glory of God is revealed. At death, Christ gives up the spirit for the world, and water flows from his side for its cleansing, but his physical nature (exceptionally) is not given back to the energy of the universe; it passes from the world and returns to the Father in glory.

And yet death is necessary, as creation itself bears witness: 'unless a grain of wheat falls to the ground and dies. . .' In the Gospel, Jesus' death is fruitful, but only because Jesus accomplishes all that the Father has given him to do. His sacrifice is the culmination of a long struggle with cosmic powers. Christ finally defeats evil by inviting it to destroy his body. He catalyses Judas' betrayal by inviting him to decide against his welcome and when Satan has entered him he says – to Judas, or Satan? – 'What you are going to do, do quickly' (13:27). Then he goes on to speak of a victory that is as surely won as his Passion is now sealed (13:31ff). Christ knows that he must lay down his life for the sheep when the wolf attacks. When evil comes to claim him he steps forward in full awareness to meet it (18:4). Evil can only be defeated by its place in the world being occupied by God himself. The cross is both the place where evil takes Jesus and the throne from which Jesus displaces evil. There death's poison and its antidote mix in one person as Christ is lifted up like the serpent in the desert (3:14). *His* death, because it is the end of *his* life, can be the unique and supreme self-offering of obedience, knowledge and love to the Father, a vicious and unjust death born for the sake of those who face death fearing suffering and feeling the weight of wickedness in the world. The light shines in the darkness for those threatened by darkness.

This victory of love, of submission, of crucifixion, is the only victory Christ wins. Victory is an emotive word indeed, and we should be mindful that to the woman's exclamation,

'What a glorious thing must be a victory, Sir', Wellington replied, 'The greatest tragedy in the world, Madam, except a defeat'.[4] John, however, does not in any sense make the glory of victory a literary sequel to the tragedy of the cross. For him, no darkness gathers over the land when Jesus is crucified (cf. Mark 15:33). The cross *is* the glory of God, because it is where Christ lays down his life freely to reveal the full extent of divine love. There in the flesh he consecrates himself to the truth, in love, prayer, offering, crucifixion. As Michael Ramsay expresses it, 'Calvary is no disaster which needs the Resurrection to reverse it, but a victory so signal that the Resurrection follows quickly to seal it'.[5]

John wants his readers to see in the dignity and majesty of Christ's sacrifice a unique revelation of the truth (18:14): he consecrates himself but needs to consecrate his followers (17:19); he invites evil to come upon himself but his disciples need to be sheltered from it (18:8). Nonetheless the victory of the cross is won by the Word made flesh, by grace; and just as the life of a child of God is lived by grace in the flesh, so also John wants to reveal to all who have faith the possibility of a kingly death. The truth, the realm into which the crucified Christ has entered fully by his obedience, is open to all to share by faith. This argument sheds further light on the discussion of ecstasy in Chapters 4 and 5 which there we described in personal terms. We see the cosmic import of the laying down of life: it is the way that the world's egocentricity is defeated by obedience; it is the way that love can gather up the scattered fragments of the world's truth into unity in a crucified body and there be offered to the Father. Evil is overcome in the embrace of death. John is saying that the cross is not something that people have to go through to get resurrected; it is the place where, in Christ, each person can find the final answer to Pilate's question, 'What is truth?'

Prophetic Aspects of Passion

The world is judged by the truth that the Passion reveals. Our society remains ill at ease with death, able to tolerate its happening unobtrusively in hospitals but unable to affirm its meaning for life. Anthony Bloom has on many occasions spoken against a people who live provisionally because they do not acknowledge the imminence of death. The common man and woman of post-Christian society believe in a heaven where autonomous human activities can resume happily after the disruption of suffering, in a heaven without God.[6] How different from the victory of the cross, the heaven of complete trust in the Father and of joy transcending all evil. It seems a folly in this world to proclaim that dying can be clothed in hope and peace rather than hedged about by remorse and sorrow. The world's folly is greater, though, and is revealed wherever the defences of heavenly hope are stripped bare. Then there remains only a good night of extinction, the end of regret in darkness:

> Do not go gentle into that good night,
> Old age should burn and rave at close of day;
> Rage, rage against the dying of the light.
>
> Though wise men at their end know dark is right,
> Because their words had forked no lightning they
> Do not go gentle into that good night.[7]

We cannot help but be impressed by this invocation of the human spirit to battle against its inevitable destiny, so showing the mettle of its years, but the grieving Dylan Thomas has set a cruel test for his father. If dying is judged by the measure of the ferocity of the struggle for life, then death itself can only ever be a defeat. The poem turns out to be a foolish grasping at the straws of mortality, a pointless demand to hold onto an unfinished and unfinishable existence. The trouble in practice is that the dying often do not have the energy to fight; death draws a white sheet quietly over tiredness. This heroic view of dying is as hard to sustain in the face of the evidence as the denial of death.

The heroism of letting go which we considered in Chapters 4 and 5 was not supposed to suggest the spectacular. A good death is prosaic but none the less truthful for that, as a tale from the Desert Fathers can help us to realise:

> The story is told that one of the elders lay dying in Scete, and the brethren surrounded his bed, dressed him in the shroud, and began to weep. But he opened his eyes and laughed. He laughed another time, and then a third time. When the brethren saw this, they asked him, saying: Tell us, Father, why are you laughing while we weep? He said to them: I laughed the first time because you fear death. I laughed the second time because you are not ready for death. And the third time I laughed because from labours I go to my rest. As soon as he had said this, he closed his eyes in death.[8]

Here we have a man – rather shockingly – mocking the world as he dies. His is the victory, though his friends fail to share it. He bears witness to what, through his life of prayer, is intensely and personally his in his dying. The story bears witness to the possibility that death can be overcome; the disciples stand by helplessly in the story, yet the story continues to be told so that they, too, may learn to chuckle from their deathbed. In our time, when stories like this do seem ludicrous to many, it is right to press Pilate's question. Perhaps it is plausible to see 'victory' in death if that death is relatively painless or comes at the end of a long and useful life; but when someone faces a painful, unnecessary or untimely death then credulity is strained.

In this book we have tried to face the truth that in history once, for eternity, a man died who faced a far more brutal and untimely death than the elder in Scete. His story continues to be told as a witness to a real possibility: that there is no force in the cosmos which can conquer divine love, even when it shares all the weakness of human flesh. We who look on as those we love die, even if they die with dignity and in peace, have real grief to face; each must win his or her own, personal victory; ecstasy is not a transferable commodity. This should not make us want to deny that God can give his story to his friends when they hear his call and follow him through death.

In this book we have told stories that bear witness that the truth still can be met at the cross, and we have others that make the possibility of victory plain in even deeper darkness. We might recall the martyrdom of Perpetua and her companions or the well-known story of Maximillian Kolbe's heroic self-offering in Auschwitz, which show that those who follow Christ are able to lay down their life freely and joyfully, thereby converting darkness into pure light.

Letting go of the self is seen in all its majesty when it occurs against a backcloth of evil and injustice, where to choose death paradoxically seems most pointless. But wherever death is entered into trustingly, in obedience to the call of Love, there victory will be won. One does not have to be a speculative theologian to see that if life has become an offering to God, then the final offering of life to God will bear fruit; once again a child of God steps into death giving up the spirit for his friends. Sister Janet CSMV testifies to this grace at the death of Mother Maribel of Wantage: 'Something happened when she died; some great release of life and power, as when the plane bursts the sound barrier, the captive ship the ice-floe, or the upthrust of spring breaks through the winter'.[9]

The saints reveal the truth as well as martyrs; even those who have no great record of godliness can pass through the judgement of suffering and be shaped by the truth, having heard their Shepherd's voice beyond their illusions. Perhaps Christ's victory shout is echoed most ordinarily in the laughter of those who have learnt that they are very clumsy mortals who court no joy by taking their afflictions too seriously.[10] A perfect response to the threat of death is not required; or to be more accurate, a perfect response is required but has already been made for our sake by God. Christ does not forbid troubled hearts but does want to speak comfort to them. The saints are only those who have realised most perfectly their own helplessness without God and who laugh the loudest.

Passion and Pastoral Care

If patients cannot always abandon themselves to their dying in the fashion of the saints, the same can also be said of pastors in their ministry. We have seen that the role of a pastor is to be a friend to the dying, to serve them by offering a love which is aware and constant, to be people who do not splay their egocentricity or raw emotion onto others out of need. They are witnesses to the truth. In word, deed and in their very being their calling is to communicate what they know of the Father. There is no need to romanticise the business of service. They are not called to imitate the patients they serve. Christ has given them an example of how to live the Passion which disciples ought to follow: 'love one another, just as I have loved you' – practically, with a towel, with water; but above all, with humility. Pastors, too, fail in their witness to the truth, sometimes through lack of courage or detachment, sometimes because their faith or strength fails them. Yet they will still be able to witness to the light. If they allow Christ to confront them, they will be able to return to the task chastened, humbler and better prepared for God to reveal his victory through them (16:33).[11]

Failure is to be expected in the cosmic battle against evil. John's Gospel does not set sin or evil at the root of disease, as do other biblical texts, but sees human weakness as the ground from which God's glory is revealed (9:2f; 11:4,17ff). Evil manifests itself in another way: Jesus says to the Jews who wilfully reject him that their father is the devil, and he refers to Judas as a devil (8:44; 6:70). The battle-lines are not set between sickness and health but between the truth and lies. As M.M. Thompson so acutely observes, 'John does not juxtapose glory and humiliation; he rather contrasts light, truth, love, and obedience – all encapsulated in the word "glory" – to darkness, falsehood, hate, and disobedience'.[12] The victory, then, is not to overcome human frailty, but to realise the truth of it, which means realising that without Christ nothing glorious ever comes out of dying. Without the wilful awareness of prayer, disease will remain in the darkness of wilful ignorance, which is a sign of the work of the Evil One.

The glory pastors may hope not to hinder, even to help, by their ministry is growth of communion, that sustaining reality of love between persons which is true yet undefinable. Communion is given through the cross and through the cross alone. There, a oneness is held between God and humanity in the person of Jesus Christ which death itself seals eternally. It is tempting for pastors to seek an expertise which bears comparison with that of the medical staff around them, to arm themselves with technique and knowledge; much harder for them to admit their folly in faith and to seek compassion, to be prepared humbly to offer every resource at their disposal to another, under the discipline of love. Even their calling to serve must become transparent. It must not remain a spiritual need craving for affirmation in response. Sanctified individualism will bear as little fruit as the ordinary variety. What matters is God's glory, discovered when pastors descend from the soap box of their competence or vocation and look instead to the One exalted on the cross. Then, through God's grace alone, belonging and believing will flow in true communion.

Communion and the Judgement of Community

The grace and truth of dying in union with Christ is felt most keenly in the community or communities in which it happens. The hospice and the family of terminally ill patients are two communities which interact in the course of care for the dying. Though this book has focussed on personal need, it has not done so to the exclusion of family. The whole emphasis on a person's story being fulfilled could be expressed, as it has been traditionally, in terms of reconciliation, with God and with others. But the hiatus of death must occasion a judgement of family relationships; ties made in life, for life, must be remade to withstand the finality of death. Part of the victory of the cross lies in the remaking of family by grace, when Christ gives his grieving followers, his mother and the beloved disciple, to each other (19:26f). Christ, fully aware that he is about to return to the Father, devotes his last moments to the forging of a new community, one which his death will prosper.

The possibility of new community is entirely necessary for the families of the dying. Relationships with 'loved ones' are often ambiguous, marked by many unlovely characteristics, such as possessiveness, anger, bitterness and jealousy. Families may choose denial as a way of dealing with death because they know that relationships are not strong or honest enough to bear much truth. Part of the work of dying well is to resolve or at least to face up to these failings. It may be that in the care of a hospice the patient discovers the love outside her family that enables her to let go. This is a judgement on the patient's natural family.

In the case of Don, for example, though he found peace through the chaplain's ministry, his wife left the hospice immediately after his death bitter that she had been cheated of time with her husband. Her peace lay in accepting God's judgement on Don's life, that it was complete and acceptable to him, and in accepting judgement on her own life, that her love was not marked with the same freedom as her dying husband's. Only by accepting this judgement would she have hope of sharing in new community, formed around the cross through the hiatus of death. Judgement of family life need not be painful, however. Those families where trusting, unpossessive relationships have flourished will discover that letting go of their loved ones will enable their receiving them back at new depth. Not only is love confirmed by Love's judgement but days, weeks and months are given for its intense cherishing and celebration within renewed community.

The hospice itself must also be judged by the opportunities it gives for truth to be disclosed in communion. Is the family being encouraged but not pressurised to face the reality of death? Are the patients' spiritual needs being met? Is there any aspect of care which has become inadequate or routine? It is a paradox that community works best when individuality is cherished. There needs to be a continual effort of awareness, as needs may be disclosed at awkward and unexpected times. The hospice will receive much praise from grateful patients

and families. Only a movement which holds firm to the highest ideals of service and which knows its own vulnerability in
the world will be able to face the judgement of success and
avoid seeking its own glory. Each death provides opportunity
for the hospice to review its practice and each review may
expose either grace or sin within community.

Community and the Judgement of Society

The hospice is a community which proclaims the truth about
human mortality to society. Those who have had little contact
with hospices imagine that they will be places of great gloom
and despair. But this is not the case. In a hospice sorrow and
joy can be expressed with equal honesty and conviction. Every
hospice aims to be a place where death can be faced and
dignity won, though success in this is not required of its
residents. In our age of fragmentation and alienation any true
community would be a prophetic body, but especially one
formed out of death. Frances Young sets out the challenge
that movements like the hospice make to the world: 'Society
measures triumph in terms of preserving life at all costs,
developing full potential, overcoming the odds. But might not
the real triumph be the ability to receive from one another,
to discover interdependence, to find values which make success and death equally irrelevant?'[13] If hospices are true to
their calling to love the dying their common life will point to
the triumph of the cross.

Self-giving love cannot be confined to the community in
which it is embodied. In his book *Moderated Love* Alistair
Campbell asks whether love can have any political impact.[14]
He outlines Niebuhr's three-part answer to the question:
Christian love constantly points to the 'impossible possibility'
of self-giving love; it judges society by showing how far it falls
short of true community; and it undercuts nationalism by its
demand for the forgiveness of enemies and the abandoning of
prejudice. But the impact of the hospice movement offers a
much more direct and particular challenge to society's values
than Niebuhr's words suggest, because it is a secular insti-

tution which exists in the world and which must justify to the world the expense of its existence and expansion, rubbing shoulders with government and the medical establishment in the process.

Sheila Cassidy, a doctor and medical director of a hospice, is well placed to speak out for her community in the world of politics, campaigning for the needs of the group in society with the least potential of all, the dying. More especially, she has a particular mission to the medical profession to which she belongs. In Chapter 2 of *Sharing the Darkness* she gives a fine diagnosis of the ideology and practice of mainstream medical care. She recognises that 'as doctors we are trained from the cradle to fight disease and to save life. It is instinctive, deep rooted, second nature. Disease is the enemy and death the ultimate disaster'.[15] The victory medicine seeks is the victory of prolongation of life, until nothing more can be done. So doctors become trapped into keeping people alive who wish they were not. The relationship between doctor and patient, cramped by the search for efficiency in health care, is kept formalised and contained by a busy professional who has not the time or energy to meet those who suffer on their territory.

The hospice is a community whose spokesmen and women can say that this need not be the way. Patients should be treated as people. Their place of death should be a home to them. They need to be informed about their illness and be given a share in the decisions made about its treatment. They need friends who will love and understand their fears and weakness and stand by them when they can do no more to help. Their spokesmen and women will have an impact in the world because in the hospice the quality of care they proclaim can be seen as a *possible* possibility, as Frances Young puts it, 'a microcosm of what society might be'.[16] Results are coming slowly, because the cost to society is not just money but an admission that the dying are of value to society because they are us, showing us our human need and true nature.

> We are made of dust, we are
> Flying on every wind,

> Blown to the back of the earth,
> Stormed at, broken, defiled.
> We are people of dust
> But dust with a living mind.
> Dust with a spirit, grace
> Goes to the end of the earth,
> Follows the dark act, the thought
> Lying, wounding, distraught,
> We are dust from our birth
> But in that dust is wrought
>
> A place for visions, a hope
> That reaches beyond the stars,
> Conjures and pauses the seas,
> Dust discovers our own
> Proud, torn destinies.
> Yes, we are dust to the bone.[17]

The only way to see the proper value of the dying is by facing the illusions that have led modern Western society to fear death. We do not become living people solely by the pursuit of happiness, success or independence, but by finding the God who became dust in Jesus Christ, who by holding fast to the Father through Calvary's storm drew dust into glory. Society stands to be swept away by the winds of untruth wherever it organises itself around principles of pride. It must learn to share in the suffering and death of its members if it wishes to be made regenerate by the vision of God's glory in community.

God's Glory – at the End as in the Beginning

I have tried to show the way truth can spread by judgement between patients who die well and pastors who seek communion with them, and between the communion people discover in a hospice and the community itself, and between the hospice community and society at large. There are no causal connections between these groups; bridges are made and crossed by the Spirit who is given so that Christ may be glorified in his death. Pastors reading this book would be right to see their place within this outpouring of grace as a small one. There is no room for pride; none, equally, for despair. The calling John offers is as witness to the light which is coming into the world. It is all grace when witness bursts the runnels of love lying hidden in the hearts of the proud and victory is won.

In the end, though, God's glory is beyond even human communion, for quite apart from his witnesses God meets his creation and gives it glory through the risen body of Jesus; and those pastors who find themselves with God when in communion with others must, all the more, find time to be alone with him, to contemplate their own mortality and to wonder at the world which he enters in Spirit to bestow on each and every child of his a love stronger than death. Wherever they are, pastors must stand apart to be met by eternal truth, as did Teilhard de Chardin in the Ordos desert on the Feast of Transfiguration:

> If the Fire has come down into the heart of the world it is, in the last resort, to lay hold on me and to absorb me. Henceforth I cannot be content simply to contemplate it or, by my steadfast faith, to intensify its ardency more and more in the world around me. What I must do, when I have taken part with all my energies in the consecration which causes its flames to leap forth, is to consent to the communion which will enable it to find in me the food it has come in the last resort to seek.
>
> So, my God, I prostrate myself before your presence in the universe which has now become living flame: beneath the lineaments of all that I shall encounter this day, all that happens to me, all that I achieve, it is you I desire, you I await.[18]

NOTES

Preface

1. Julia Gatta, *The Pastoral Art* (DLT, 1986), p. 111.

Chapter 1: The Journey in Time to Eternity

1. The views of Bernard, Lindars and Dodd, cited by K. Leech, *True God* (Sheldon, 1985), p. 90.
2. See R.E. Brown, *The Gospel According to John, Vol. 1* (Anchor Bible, Geoffrey Chapman, 1971), p. 23.
3. P. Evdokimov, *The Art of the Icon: A Theology of Beauty* (Anthony Clarke, 1990), pp. 127ff.
4. Lesslie Newbigin, *The Light has Come* (Handsel, 1982), p. 5.
5. The word 'now' is used twenty-seven times by John, and 'hour' twenty-five times; for this statistic and further insights into time and eternity in the Gospel I am indebted to Dr George Bebawi.
6. R.E. Brown, op. cit., p. 132.
7. See H. Nouwen, *Behold the Beauty of the Lord: Praying with Icons* (Ave Maria Press, 1987), Chapter 1; P. Evdokimov, op. cit., pp. 243ff.
8. Jung, quoted in C. Bryant, *Jung and the Christian Way* (DLT, 1983), pp. 27f.
9. J.D. Zizoulas, *Being as Communion: Studies in Personhood and the Church* (DLT, 1985), p. 46.
10. P. Brockelman, *Time and Self: Phenomenological Explorations* (American Academy of Religion, 1985), p. 22.
11. Philip Larkin, 'Dockery and Son', in *Collected Poems* (Faber and Faber, 1988).
12. P. Brockelman, op. cit., p. 39.
13. P. Evdokimov, op. cit., p. 128.
14. C.K. Barrett, *The Gospel According to St John* (SPCK, 2nd ed., 1978), pp. 205f.

15. The psychologist Colin Murray Parkes has often observed how living in the here-and-now relieves the struggle for life.

16. S. Pattison, *A Critique of Pastoral Care* (SCM, 1988), p. 106. The silence has since been broken by A.C. Thiselton who devotes the last two chapters of his book *New Horizons in Hermeneutics* (Harper Collins, 1992), some fifty pages, to the hermeneutics of pastoral theology. His work focusses on the business of reading texts in relation to varied and particular pastoral situations.

17. Ibid., p. 107.

18. Ibid., p. 131.

19. Ibid., p. 130.

20. Ibid., p. 122.

21. A.V. Campbell, *Rediscovering Pastoral Care* (DLT, 1981/6), p. 18.

22. Ibid., p. 25.

23. Ibid., p. 22.

24. Ibid., p. 24.

25. Pattison, op. cit., p. 123.

26. *Hebrews 1–8* (Word, 1991), p. clv.

27. See Pattison, op. cit., Chapter 1.

28. Ibid., p. 13.

29. Quoted in E.L. Mascall, *Whatever Happened to the Human Mind* (SPCK, 1980), p. 149.

Chapter 2: Making Space for Meeting – Pastoral Attitudes

1. W.H. Vanstone, *Love's Endeavour, Love's Expense* (DLT, 1977), p. 113.

2. C. Causley, 'Ten Types of Hospital Visitor', in *Collected Poems 1951–1975* (Papermac, 1983).

3. J.D.G. Dunn, *Jesus and the Spirit* (SCM, 1975), p. 356.

4. See, for example, R.E. Brown, *The Gospel According to John, Vol. 1* (Geoffrey Chapman, 1966), p. lxxviii. The Gospel also has a related, polemical purpose, to proclaim the truth of Christ in the face of persecution.

5. *Pace* C.K. Barrett, *The Gospel According to St John* (SPCK, 1978), p. 58.

6. Cf. G. Wainwright's views on credal belief, *Doxology: A Systematic Theology* (Epworth, 1980), p. 191.

7. R.E. Brown, op. cit., p. 24.

8. C.K. Barrett's translation, op. cit., p. 240.

9. The woman's leaving behind of the water jar signifies that her request at verse 15 for living water has been met.

10. W.H. Vanstone, *The Stature of Waiting* (DLT, 1982), Chapter 3.

11. 'Helplessness and Hope', p. 2; this short paper appears to be extracted from B.D. Rumbold's book by that title (SCM, 1986).

12. E.N. Jackson, *Counselling the Dying* (SCM, 1982), p. 159.

13. E. Kübler-Ross, *On Death and Dying* (Tavistock, 1970), p. 240.

14. In *The Oxford Book of Twentieth Century English Verse* (OUP, 1973).

15. Identified in the previous verse as the place of bodily lowliness.

16. T.F. Torrance, *Trinitarian Faith* (T & T Clark, 1988), pp. 149ff; cf. Aristotle, 'If one party stands at a vast remove, as God does, there can be no question of friendship', quoted in S. McFague, *Models of God* (SCM, 1987), p. 158.

17. B.D. Rumbold, op. cit., p. 1.

18. Cf. P. Evdokimov, *The Sacrament of Love: The Nuptial Mystery in the Light of the Orthodox Tradition* (SVS Press, 1985), p. 114: 'If one were to stand outside the Incarnation, the infinite, qualitative, unbridgeable distance between man and God, His absolute otherness, it would make love unhappy and all communion, even communication, indirect and veiled.'

19. J.A. Baker, 'Why Should this Happen to Me?' (Address given at St Christopher's Hospice, Oct. 1987), p. 13.

20. See B. Hebblethwaite, *The Incarnation: Collected Essays in Christology* (CUP, 1987), p. 157.

21. W.H. Vanstone, *Love's Endeavour, Love's Expense*, p. 50.

22. 'Christianity and the Ideal of Detachment', 1988 Frank Lake Memorial Lecture (Lingdale Papers 12, Clinical Theology Association, 1989), p. 3.

23. Most notably J. Moltmann; see *The Crucified God* (SCM, 1974), pp. 267ff.

24. W. Carr, *The Pastor as Theologian: The Integration of Pastoral Ministry, Theology and Discipleship* (SPCK, 1989), p. 87.

25. Ibid., p. 85.

26. Ibid., p. 88.

27. Ibid., p. 95.

28. Quoted in A.V. Campbell, *Moderated Love* (SPCK, 1984), p. 105.

29. And dangerous for the patient too, because it encourages dependency.

30. *Rediscovering Pastoral Care* (DLT, 1981/6), p. 42.

31. Ibid., p. 11.

32. Ibid., p. 34.

33. Ibid., p. 39.

34. Ibid., p. 92.

35. In *One Minute Wisdom* (Image, 1985), p. 10.

36. In *Studies in Pastoral Theology and Social Anthropology* (University of Birmingham, 1986), p. 57.
37. *Awareness* (Fount, 1990), p. 167.
38. The title of Rowan Williams' fine book on spirituality, derived from the poetry of R.S. Thomas.
39. Quoted in J.V. Taylor, *A Matter of Life and Death* (SCM, 1986), pp. 46f.
40. *Famous Prayers* (Lion, 1983), p. 68.

Chapter 3: Building Communion – Pastoral Acts

1. R. Schnackenburg, *The Gospel According to St John, Vol. 3* (Cross-road, 1987), p. 392.
2. The trend has always been stronger in the US than in Britain and has been countered there in polemic fashion by T. Oden.
3. See, for example, K. Leech, *Silence and Ministry* (SLG, 1987).
4. 'East Coker III', in *The Complete Poems and Plays of T.S. Eliot* (Faber and Faber, 1966).
5. See A. Louf, *Teach Us to Pray* (DLT, 1974/91), Chapter 4.
6. Ibid., p. 40.
7. See A.V. Campbell, *Moderated Love*, p. 110.
8. N. Autton, *Touch: An Exploration* (DLT, 1989), p. 117.
9. Ibid., p. 119.
10. See Chapter 5, 'Eternal Life and the End of Suffering', for a synthesis of these two aspects of the importance of the body.
11. See Elizabeth Jennings' fascinating poem, 'Identity', *Collected Poems* (Carcanet, 1986).
12. P. Evdokimov, *The Sacrament of Love*, p. 112.
13. Ibid., p. 96.
14. I. de la Potterie, *The Hour of Jesus: The Passion and Resurrection of Jesus According to John: Text and Spirit* (St Paul, 1989), p. 12.
15. *Rediscovering Pastoral Care*, p. 16.
16. 'There is a silence which is the result of awkwardness, of uncertainty, of a sense of our rootlessness. There is angry silence. There is a silence of coldness, of fermenting resentment and cruelty', K. Leech, op. cit., p. 2.
17. From 'The Discernment of Stirrings' by the author of *The Cloud of Unknowing*.
18. *Love's Endeavour, Love's Expense*, p. 107.
19. E. Jennings, *Selected Poems* (Carcanet, 1979/1985).
20. I. de la Potterie, op. cit., pp. 94f.
21. The pastor practises the Christian virtue of 'fitting in'; see J.V. Taylor, *A Matter of Life and Death* (SCM, 1986), p. 75.

22. J.D. Zizoulas, *Being as Communion: Studies in Personhood and the Church* (DLT, 1985), p. 105.
23. See A.V. Campbell, *Moderated Love*, p. 96.
24. Quoted in B.D. Rumbold, *Helplessness and Hope: Pastoral Care in Terminal Illness* (SCM, 1986), p. 52, and also in Campbell, *Rediscovering Pastoral Care*, p. 43.
25. Campbell, ibid., p. 12.
26. In the manner of a 'fool', ibid., p. 50.
27. A better term than the over-used 'authentic': the word is not just existentially and individually true but has eternal value as coming from the Source of life.
28. Campbell, op. cit., p. 44.
29. Rumbold, op. cit., p. 69.
30. The summary is drawn from Rumbold, op. cit., pp. 61ff.
31. S. Cassidy, *Sharing the Darkness: The Spirituality of Caring* (DLT, 1988), pp. 74f.
32. Mother Mary Clare SLG, *Encountering the Depths* (DLT, 1981), p. 49.
33. Published in the 'Witness' column of the *Church Times*.

Chapter 4: Suffering and Salvation – The Gift Offered

1. See Chapter 3, the discussion on speaking the truth in love.
2. E. Kübler-Ross, *On Death and Dying* (Tavistock, 1970), p. 17.
3. E. Käsemann, *The Testament of Jesus: A Study of the Gospel of John in the Light of Chapter 17* (SCM, 1968), p. 9.
4. J.V. Taylor, *A Matter of Life and Death*, p. 40.
5. I. de la Potterie, *The Hour of Jesus*, p. 120.
6. Ibid., p. 15.
7. P. Evdokimov, *The Sacrament of Love*, p. 50.
8. H. Ward, *Giving Yourself Away* (Grove, Spirituality No. 26, 1988), p. 15.
9. P. Larkin, 'Faith Healing', in *Collected Poems* (Faber and Faber, 1988), p. 126.
10. P.E. Irion, *Hospice and Ministry* (Abingdon, 1988), p. 22.
11. H.U. von Balthasar, in *The von Balthasar Reader*, eds. M. Kehland and W. Löser (Crossroad, 1982), p. 65.
12. Ibid., p. 85, my emphasis.

Chapter 5: Victory through Death – The Gift Received

1. See A. Nygren, *Eros and Agape* (SPCK, 1953), though Nygren himself modified his position later. The mystics of course had no such inhibitions; cf. Mother Julian's words from God: 'I am

he who makes you to love; I am he who makes you to long; I am he, the endless fulfilling of all true desires', *Showings*, Chapter 59.

2. See K. Leech, *Soul Friend* (Sheldon, 1977), Chapter 1.

3. Augustine, *Confessions*, Book 1.

4. This becomes a *frightening* reality in the West between the sixteenth and eighteenth centuries; see P. Ariès, *Western Attitudes Towards Death* (Marion Boyars, 1974), p. 58.

5. I. Ainsworth-Smith and P. Speck, *Letting Go: Caring for the Dying and the Bereaved* (SPCK, 1982), p. 35.

6. J.V. Taylor calls it, somewhat inaccurately, 'a principle of all existence', *A Matter of Life and Death*, p. 61. See Chapter 7, 'The Necessity of Death'.

7. Ibid., p. 65.

8. T.S. Eliot, 'Little Gidding IV', in *The Complete Poems and Plays of T.S. Eliot* (Faber and Faber, 1966).

9. Within the acknowledgement that life is a gift a person can still, in appreciation of the gift, put up a healthy fight for life, preparing for eternity by 'living it up . . . giving the most to life and getting the most from it, while it is on offer' (J.A.T. Robinson, preaching when terminally ill).

10. P. Sheldrake, *Images of Holiness* (DLT, 1987), p. 37.

11. B.D. Rumbold, *Helplessness and Hope*, p. ix.

12. Ibid., p. 68.

13. Rumbold discusses grace on pp. 42 and 51ff.

14. A. de Mello, *The Song of the Bird* (Doubleday, 1982), pp. 99f.

15. P. Evdokimov, *The Sacrament of Love*, p. 53.

16. Ibid., p. 19f: 'the flesh is the biosphere where the spirit becomes incarnate when offered to its transfiguring powers; indeed it is the open tomb where the spirit buries itself alive.'

17. P. Teilhard de Chardin, 'The Mass on the World', in *Hymn of the Universe* (Collins, 1965), p. 26.

18. God's love does not by nature need a response but it seeks a response so that his joy may be completed in his creatures.

19. 'East Coker III', op. cit., p. 181.

20. H.U. von Balthasar, *Mysterium Paschale* (T & T Clark), p. 258.

21. In the New Testament *agape* usually, but not always, means divine love; see Bruce, *Galatians* (Paternoster, 1982), pp. 251f.

22. This is to have the insights of the feminist critique of traditional spirituality in mind, which argues that a sin of woman is to accept identity as a non-person, a servant of her male oppressor.

23. H. Ward, *Giving Yourself Away*, p. 17.

24. T.S. Eliot, 'Little Gidding V'. Teilhard de Chardin's vision for the future union of creation with Christ has been called optimistic, but yet it is founded on 'a sort of reversal, a turning about, an *excentration*, which must involve the temporary collapse not merely of all individual achievements but even of everything that looks like an advancement for humanity', op. cit., p. 30.
25. In *The Oxford Book of Prayer* (Oxford, 1985), p. 131.
26. See Chapter 1, the story of Albert.
27. The aim of saying the Jesus Prayer also corresponds to the needs of those who suffer spiritually: 'Our heart is to absorb the Lord and the Lord to absorb our heart, and the two are to become one', A Monk of the Eastern Church (Lev Gillett), *The Jesus Prayer* (SVS Press, 1987), p. 50.
28. Quoted by J.R.H. Moorman, in *The Study of Spirituality* (SPCK, 1986), p. 307.
29. W.H. Vanstone, *Love's Endeavour, Love's Expense*, p. 96.
30. Jacopone, quoted by J.R.H. Moorman, op. cit., p. 307.
31. See J.A. Baker, 'Why Should This Happen to Me?' (Address given at St Christopher's Hospice, Dec. 1987).
32. Cf. J. Moltmann, *The Open Church* (SCM, 1978), p. 57, 'In the fellowship of Jesus [God's children] no longer experience God as Lord, nor only as Father; rather they experience him in his innermost nature as Friend.'
33. W.H. Vanstone, op. cit., p. 45.
34. H.U. von Balthasar, *The von Balthasar Reader*, p. 66.
35. See esp. S. Pattison, *A Critique of Pastoral Care*, Chapter 8.
36. J. Macquarrie, *Christian Hope* (Mowbray, 1978), pp. 5f.
37. C. Caretto, *Why O Lord? The Inner Meaning of Suffering* (DLT, 1986), p. 11.
38. Quoted in K. Leech, *True God*, p. 243.
39. See Chapter 1, 'Time and the Loss of Body and Mind'.
40. Minnie Louise Haskins, source untraced.

Chapter 6: Judgement

1. D. Senior and C. Stuhlmueller, *The Biblical Foundations for Mission* (SCM, 1983), p. 285. Obviously, John's use of Word christology inextricably links creation and salvation, human need and spiritual salvation.
2. L. Newbigin, *The Light has Come*, p. 112.
3. See Chapter 7.
4. John writes from a time when access to this relationship was assured.

5. See Chapter 3.
6. J.A. Baker, 'The Family and Death: A Christian Contribution' (Paper given at St Christopher's Hospice, Oct. 1987), p. 3.
7. C. Saunders, *I was Sick and you Visited Me* (reprinted from *In the Service of Medicine*), p. 3.
8. E. Muir, *Collected Poems* (Faber and Faber, 1984).
9. T.F. Torrance, *The Trinitarian Faith*, p. 53.
10. C. Saunders, op. cit., p. 1.
11. G. Mursell, *Out of the Deep: Prayer as Protest* (DLT, 1989), see especially Chapter 10.
12. G. Wainwright, *Doxology*, p. 446.
13. J.B. Torrance, in *The Incarnation: Ecumenical Studies in the Nicene-Constantinopolitan Creed* (Handsel, 1981), p. 142.
14. A.V. Campbell, *Rediscovering Pastoral Care*, p. 65.
15. See Chapter 3.
16. In *Collected Poems*.
17. *Love's Endeavour, Love's Expense*, p. 44.
18. George Macdonald, in *The Sun, Dancing* (Puffin, 1984), p. 24.

Chapter 7: The Glory of God and the Salvation of the World

1. T.S. Eliot, 'Little Gidding V', op. cit.
2. This phrase derives from Orthodox trinitarian tradition where the Father has been seen as Love crucifying and the Son Love crucified.
3. J. Bowker, *The Meanings of Death* (Cambridge, 1991), p. 220.
4. The caution and quotation both come from personal correspondence with Canon Stephen Platten, to whom I am grateful for comments on Chapter 4 of this book.
5. A.M. Ramsey, *The Glory of God and the Transfiguration of Christ* (Longmans, 1949), p. 81.
6. Canon Henry Scott Holland's meditation, much used at funerals, 'Death is Nothing at All', which does its mawkish best to reinforce this fantasy, glosses over the hiatus of death altogether: 'Life means all that it ever meant. It is the same as it ever was; there is unbroken continuity.'
7. Dylan Thomas, 'Do Not Go Gentle into that Good Night', in *The Oxford Book of Twentieth Century English Verse* (OUP, 1973).
8. In Merton, *The Wisdom of the Desert* (Darley Anderson, 1988), pp. 49f.
9. *Mother Maribel of Wantage* (SPCK, 1973), p. ix.
10. See S. Pattison, *A Critique of Pastoral Care*, Chapter 8.
11. Ibid., Chapter 7, esp. pp. 160ff.

12. M.M. Thompson, *The Humanity of Jesus in the Fourth Gospel* (Fortress, 1988), p. 112.
13. F. Young, *Face to Face: A Narrative Essay in the Theology of Suffering* (T & T Clark, 1990), p. 110.
14. Campbell, op. cit., p. 121.
15. Cassidy, op. cit., p. 15.
16. Young, op. cit., p. 115.
17. E. Jennings, 'Dust', in *Collected Poems*, p. 212.
18. 'The Mass on the World: Communion', in *Hymn of the Universe* (Collins, 1961), p. 29.